THE LITTLE BOOK
OF REVOLUTION

THE LITTLE BOOK
OF REVOLUTION
A Distributive Strategy
for Democracy

David Akadjian

Published by David Akadjian LLC, Cincinnati, OH.

Cover art by Maiez Mehdi.
Edited by Mollie Brumm.

A special thanks to the following for their advice and encouragement:

My mom, my dad (who passed away too soon), Brad Prescott, Glenna Rust, Chris Weigant, Bruce Levine, Laura Providenti, Kit Burns, Coulter Loeb, Julie Ladd, Mark Andersen from Daily Kos, Susan Forman, Trevor Cessna, John Stoehr from The Washington Spectator, Mike Gibboney, Jilly Baker-Gibboney, Brian Griffin, Kevin Bard, Jeff and Aimee Boley, Jason and Michelle Moseley, Ryan Meyer, Ann Kruetzkamp, John Schaffer, Anita Antoninka, Nathan Lane, Alli Hammond, Steve and Lisa Nicholson, Ian Young, Tom Brooke, Vanessa Holtkamp, Stephen Whitson, Elise Maynard, Andrew Higley, Nicole Zappanti, Gregg Wilson, Emily Rockenfelder Wilson, Charyl Mikles, Joe Suer, Don Rucknagel, Plan Cincinnati, Gavin Devore Leonard and the One Ohio Now team, Zach Schiller and the Policy Matters Ohio team, Paul Hogarth, the entire Daily Kos community, Believe in Cincinnati, Paul Brumm and the Sexy Time Live Karaoke band for the best damn karaoke around.

Library of Congress Cataloging-in-Publication Data:

The Little Book of Revolution: A Distributive Strategy for Democracy / David Akadjian.

    p. cm.

    "David Akadjian, LLC."

    Includes bibliographical references and index.

    ISBN 978-0-692-22034-4

    Library of Congress Control Number: 2014911732

Printed in the United States of America.

10 9 8 7 6 5 4 3 2 1

To TK

*For encouraging
me to do this*

*and all of the
wonderful people*

*who've helped
along the way*

CONTENTS

  11.1   What does "influencing without authority" mean?   193
  11.2   How do we judge character?   195
  11.3   The right/left game revisited   199
  11.4   Metaphoric relationships   199
  11.5   Heroes and villains   201
  11.6   When talent and point of pride intersect   202
  11.7   How does this relate to political discussions?   205
  11.8   Ground rules   207
          Practice   208

12   Common denominators in corporate framing   **211**

  12.1   Limiting options   213
          12.1.1   Creating space   214
  12.2   "Good" people vs. "bad" people   218
          12.2.1   Expanding the definition of "good" people 219
  12.3   Telling only part of the story   221
          12.3.1   Expanding conceptual frames   223
          Practice   224

13   Overcoming objections   **225**

  13.1   Objections are expressions of emotional need   226
  13.2   What to do if someone treats you like an enemy   230
  13.3   Win the audience   231
          Practice   232

PART V   CLOSE

14   A virtual union   **237**

  14.1   A recent experience   238
  14.2   What unites us   243
  14.3   Key takeaways and actions   245

A   References and Index   **250**

          About the Author   250
          Contact   252

PREFACE

Multivariate analysis indicates that economic elites and organized groups representing business interests have substantial independent impacts on U.S. government policy, while average citizens and mass-based interest groups have little or
no independent influence.

—Martin Gilens and Benjamin I. Page [Gil14]

Recently, a study by Martin Gilens and Benjamin Page at Princeton University concluded what everyone already knew: the United States is not a
democracy, it's an oligarchy responsive mainly to a powerful elite.

No surprise. Everyone I know across the political spectrum, Republicans,
Democrats, and Independents, knew this already. The study is one of several
confirming what we've been seeing for years.

I bring this up because often we tend to think that if only people knew, things would be different. If only we could get them the right information. If only we could "wake them up."

Sooner or later, we're going to have to face what's staring us in the face: the issue isn't that people don't know.

The issue is: What to do about it?

People are frustrated with the political system because, as Gilens and Page point out, it's not responding well to public interests. Republicans play to the cultural issues of white, rural, and suburban voters to get elected and then serve corporate interests. Democrats play to the cultural interests of urban, academic, and minority voters to get elected and then often serve corporate interests.

Third parties have been unable to gain traction.

Each time we seem to find a truly populist leader or group, like Howard Dean or the Occupy movement, the same economic elites and business interests quickly work to discredit or marginalize them.

If a strategy is going to succeed, it's going to have to be a distributed strategy. It will have to have many leaders or be virtually leaderless. You may think this sounds impossible, but here's some quick math that may convince you otherwise.

Consider a duplicable strategy where each person convinces 20 people within his or her immediate circle:

- 1st round = 20 people

- 2nd round = 400 people

- 3rd round = 8,000 people

- 4th round = 160,000 people

- 5th round = 3,200,000 people

- 6th round = 64,000,000 people

Quickly, we would have a significant voting bloc.

Not only that, but in a distributed strategy, each round develops a sizable number of leaders (from the the previous round). At round 5, for example, 160,000 leaders exist from round 4.

So we can make excuses or we can realize that we're six rounds away from reaching 64 million people.

The question then is, what to teach, what to propagate?

Corporations have spent inordinate amounts of money during the past 40 years winning people over by developing a set of core beliefs and teaching people how to talk about them.

We, the people, have better beliefs and a better story, we just don't have a focused strategy and the appropriate tools for winning people over.

Does this mean we need to do what corporations have been doing?

No. In fact, often this is the problem. We try to play the same game as corporate interest groups, and, as Gilens and Page point out, we lose.

Corporations use a top-down, divide-and-conquer approach. Our approach needs to be different. It needs to be bottom-up, inclusive, and, I believe, distributive.

This book is an attempt at such a distributive strategy—easy to learn, implement, and teach.

It's a guide to help you have better political conversations. Why doesn't the "truth" work? How do people think about politics? What strategies are being used by corporate interest groups? What values do we have in common?

Most importantly, what can each of us personally do to shift the direction of change?

I've watched some of my political friends engage in terrible, emotionally draining fights with people who could very easily be their allies. When I asked them about their conversations, they'd typically say the other person just "doesn't get it" or something similar.

Is this true? In my experience, it isn't. People do get that our country isn't a democracy and that our government primarily serves the interests of the wealthy. Why is it so difficult then to change?

Here, we'll look at some of the reasons and what we can personally do.

The question that interests me most is, what has the biggest impact? If each of us could pitch in a little bit each day or each week, what would make the biggest difference?

Some of the answers I found not only surprised me, but were very much different than what I was used to doing. I also learned that it is possible to talk about politics with just about anyone without killing myself (or others).

If we can fight better fights, not only will we be more successful, but we'll also be much happier and not nearly as frustrated.

We can also change the landscape so that political parties must move to match.

I've included ideas for practicing at the end of each chapter to make the book as useful as possible. I've also included examples and conversations from my own personal experience to demonstrate that not only can it be done, but that it's easier than you might think.

This book is what I put together for my first 20 friends.

Enjoy!

DAVID AKADJIAN

September 2014

PART I

THE SITUATION

CHAPTER 1

WHY THOMAS PIKETTY WON'T SAVE US

If the human brain were so simple that we could understand it, we would be so simple that we couldn't.

—Emerson Pugh as quoted in *The Biological Origin of Human Values.* [Pug77]

1.1 The mind doesn't work the way we think it does

In a computer architecture class, a professor of mine once remarked offhandedly that people throughout history have described how our own minds work using the most complex piece of technology we've created to date.

Because we have to describe our minds without knowing exactly how they work, we choose technologies we've developed as metaphors and models for the mind.

I found this comment much more interesting than the lecture on computer architecture because it opened up some very interesting questions.

How do the assumptions we make about how our minds work impact:

- How we view the world?

- How we teach and learn?

- How we go about our day-to-day lives?

Much more specifically though, the way we conceptualize our minds has a tremendous influence on how we talk about some of our most relevant issues. I'll call these issues political issues. But that is probably not the best way to characterize them. At heart, they are moral issues.

How you ever spoken with someone about a particular issue and wondered why the person just didn't seem to get it? Why do we have maxims about avoiding religious and political discussions? Why does talking about politics make us so angry?

Why do so many of our efforts at truth-telling fail? And is there anything we can do about it?

These are the questions I've been asking myself and trying to figure out with my friends, family, and acquaintances for years.

What I've found is that the mind doesn't work the way we think it does.

And the way we think about how we think often leads us astray when it comes to political discussions.

1.2   Metaphors for the mind

In the 5th century B.C., the mind was viewed as a hydraulic system based on the development of aqueducts in Ancient Greece [Dau01].

The Greek philosopher Hippocrates, for example, believed there were four basic humours: black bile, yellow bile, phlegm, and blood. When the humours were out of balance, it was believed, people would get sick. The humors were also linked to personality types and moods such as sanguine, choleric, melancholic, and phlegmatic, apathetic.

Melan chole literally means "black bile" in Greek.

Figure 1.1   Moods related to the four humours. [Lav83]

In the 2nd century B.C., the Roman physician Galen evolved this model into a theory of animal spirits. In Galen's model, the brain communicated with the body using the fluid known as "animal spirits."

The liver produced natural spirits that the heart turned into vital spirits that were then sent on to the brain through the carotid arteries. The brain turned these vital spirits into animal spirits that were thought to be stored in the brain until needed by the muscles or to carry sensory impressions [Cos06].

In the 17th century, Descartes advocated a mechanical view of the universe and living organisms. Descartes believed the nervous system transported animal spirits back and forth from the body to the brain. Descartes attributed many of our experiences to the function of the body's organs as mechanical components [Des72]:

> the reception of light, sounds, odors, tastes, warmth, and other like qualities into the exterior organs of sensation; the impression of the corresponding ideas upon a common sensorium and on the imagination; the retention or imprint of these ideas in the Memory; the internal movements of the Appetites and Passions; and finally, the external motions of all the members of the body ... I wish that you would consider all of these

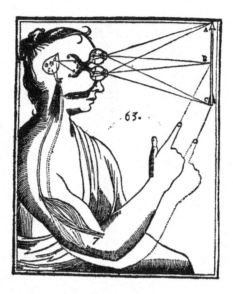

Figure 1.2   René Descartes' illustration of dualism. [Des72]

as following altogether naturally in this Machine from the disposition of
its organs alone, neither more nor less than do the movements of a clock
or other automaton from that of its counterweight and wheels

While Descartes believed the mind was ephemeral and the body mechanical
(dualism), many mechanical metaphors also arose for the mind. Clocks
were likely one of the first. You can still hear this thinking in metaphors
we use today like "you can see the wheels turning" or "she has a mind like
a clock" or "like clockwork." Though people never believed actual gears
existed in our heads, they believed that some series of actions was taking
place, even if we were unable to describe exactly how our mind machinery
worked.

John Locke visualized the mind as a *tabula rasa*, or blank piece of paper,
upon which experience left an imprint. Contrary to many before him, he
believed we weren't born with innate ideas but rather that everything we
know was shaped by our experience.

You can hear the impact of the Gutenberg printing press and printed books,
popular throughout Europe by the 17th century, on Locke's thinking about
memory [Loc97]:

The other way of retention is, the power to revive again in our minds those ideas which, after imprinting, have disappeared, or have been as it were laid aside out of sight. And thus we do, when we conceive heat or light, yellow or sweet,—the object being re-moved. This is memory, which is as it were the storehouse of our ideas.

Ideas imprint on memory like type or script on a blank sheet of paper.

It's fascinating to watch how thinking about human behavior evolved as new inventions arose and the most advanced technology of the day became metaphors for the human mind.

It's even more fascinating to think about how quaint and antiquated some of these ideas seem yet how some of the metaphorical reasoning still exists in our day-to-day conversations and thoughts. We still understand what people mean when someone is described as melancholic or sanguine, for example.

Not surprisingly then, when James Watt invented the practical steam engine in 1781, we incorporated it into our thinking about how the human mind works.

Freud, for example, believed in the conscious and the unconscious and characterized the human mind as a struggle between the two. Desires, some of which might be seen as unacceptable by society, could be suppressed or repressed. But, like steam in a steam engine, if held down psychological pressure continued to build until it found an outlet.

Sigmund Freud, writing about neuroses, said the following about hysteria [Fre89]:

Hysteria begins with the overwhelming of the ego, which is what paranoia leads to. The raising of tension at the primary experience of unpleasure is so great that the ego does not resist it and forms no psychical symptom but is obliged to allow a manifestation of discharge—usually an excessive expression of excitation.

If no immediate outlet is to be found, ideas are pushed down into the subconscious as a defense mechanism to save the ego. As ideas are pushed down, pressure builds similar to steam pressure in a steam engine. Freud believed that these internal pressures eventually released themselves in a variety of ways and lead to art, war, passion, and so on.

In the 19th century, the Jacquard loom was the most complex mechanical device invented to date. It used thousands of punched cards in order to create intricate woven patterns.

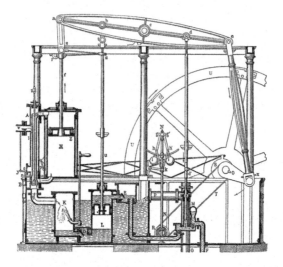

Figure 1.3   Illustration of James Watt's practical steam engine. [Wat95]

The neuroscientist Sir Charles Sherrington wrote in his 1942 book *Man on His Nature* that the mind was like an enchanted loom [Sher42]:

> The great topmost sheet of the mass, that where hardly a light had twinkled or moved, becomes now a sparkling field of rhythmic flashing points with trains of traveling sparks hurrying hither and thither. The brain is waking and with it the mind is returning. It is as if the Milky Way entered upon some cosmic dance. Swiftly the head mass becomes an enchanted loom where millions of flashing shuttles weave a dissolving pattern, always a meaningful pattern though never an abiding one; a shifting harmony of subpatterns.

Blaise Pascal constructed the first mechanical calculator capable of addition and subtraction in the 17th century.

In the 1800s, Charles Babbage designed first the difference engine, a machine for calculating the values of polynomial functions, and then a more general computational machine called the analytical engine. The analytical engine, drawing inspiration from the Jacquard loom, used punch cards as inputs for mechanical calculations.

We create new inventions and subsequently new inventions influence both how we think and future inventions. Interestingly enough, Jacquard looms still exist, though now controlled by computers.

Figure 1.4   The Jacquard loom. [Eng60]

1.3   Early electrical metaphors

Static electricity generators have existed since 1650 when Otto von Guer-
icke built the first using a sulphur ball. The Leyden jar, an early capacitor
for storing electricity, was developed in the 1700s and allowed scientists to
easily store electricity for experiments.

These inventions served little purpose outside scientific labs other than cu-
riosity; if you touched one you would receive a shock.

The shocking effect wasn't understood until the 1790s, however, when the
Italian scientist Luigi Galvani discovered that a spark caused the leg muscles of dead frogs to twitch. This discovery lead to the idea of bioelectricity.
The galvanometer, an instrument used for measuring electricity, is named
after Galvani.

With Galvani's discovery, electrical impulses began to replace water or mechanical means as a metaphor for communication between the senses and

the mind. In 1849, the German scientist Hermann von Helmholtz measured the speed at which electrical signals were carried through nerve fiber. At the time, people believed the signal was instantaneous [Gly10].

The telegraph, invented in the 1830s, provided Helmholtz a conceptual model for understanding how sensory signals reached the brain.

Figure 1.5   Seattle power, telephone, and telegraph lines, 1934. [Sea34]

Timothy Lenoir, Stanford science historian, remarked on Helmholtz's discoveries [Len94]:

> From as early as 1850 he drew analogies between the electrical telegraph and the process of perception. The telegraph began to serve as a generalized model for representing the process of sensation and perception.

Much of this work would prove prophetic as in 1952, Alan Lloyd Hodgkin and Andrew Huxley, researchers at the University of Cambridge were able to model the flow of bioelectrical current through a nerve using differential equations originally developed for undersea coaxial cable transmission

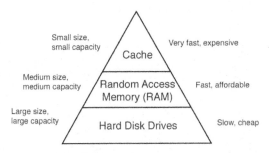

Figure 1.6   Computer memory hierarchy.

(known commonly as the telegrapher's equations). Hodgkin and Huxley won the Nobel Prize in Physiology in 1963 for their work.

Other electrical components we related to the human mind at one point or another throughout the 20th century include vacuum tubes, transistors, electrical switches, resistors, capacitors, amplifiers, relays, tape recorders, and memory banks.

1.4   The computer

Today, however, by far the most widespread metaphor for the brain is the computer.

Computer memory is a location for a binary piece of information (a 1 or a 0) that can be accessed and typically overwritten as needed with new data. We named memory chips after the term we use to describe our own recall of information.

Faster memory such as cache or random-access memory (RAM) stores current information and is located "closer" to the processor. Slower memory (hard disk memory) stores large programs and data. Programs and data are pulled into RAM/cache memory for quick access by the central processing unit (CPU) and replaced when they aren't being used. The idea is to have data that is being used most frequently in the fastest, most expensive pieces of memory—typically, cache memory.

Cache and RAM are both emptied when the computer is turned off, disk drives store memory even when the computer is turned off.

When we think of how our own memory works, we often think of our brain as accessing a specific memory area where we store and retrieve information in our minds. The concept of short-term memory is very similar to the cache/RAM memory and long-term memory is much more like a disk drive.

Similarly, we often think of our brains as having a processing unit. That is, if we feed specific data to our mind, and process it appropriately, the right answer should appear. For example, if we understand the operation called multiplication and are given two different numbers (say 7 and 6) we can return a correct result, 42. Our brains in this sense are viewed as computing machines which, if given a specific input, will produce a specific output.

Computers produce results by sending data from memory modules to the central processing unit where computation takes place and sends the results to an output device or memory.

Most people know this computer metaphor so well that if you ask them how they think the mind works, they will describe a computer.

Much of our modern day language about the mind assumes the mind as computer metaphor. When we say someone's mind is like a computer, for example, we typically mean this as a complement. It tends to mean that they have immediate access to large stores of information and are able to process data very quickly with accurate results.

John Daugman expresses this belief perfectly [Dau01]:

> Today's embrace of the computational metaphor in the cognitive and neural sciences is so widespread and automatic that it begins to appear less like an innovative leap than like a bandwagon phenomenon ... There is a tendency to rephrase every assertion about mind or brain in computational terms, even if it strains the vocabulary or requires the suspension of disbelief.

1.5   What does this have to do with Thomas Piketty?

Let's take a brief look at a few common political beliefs.

To do this, I'm going to use Thomas Piketty as an example. I could just as easily have chosen Noam Chomsky, Bernie Sanders, Sasha Abramsky, or any number of political writers.

I chose Piketty because a friend of mine believes that Piketty's book, *Capital in the Twenty-First Century*, is going to make the difference. He believes this book is going to be the one that finally wakes people out of their complacency and jars them into action.

My friend, you see, believes in the great liberal truth myth. He believes that people make decisions based on fact and available information and that if we can somehow just input the right information to people their computer minds will spit out a more correct output.

He's not alone.

Here's Ralph Nader echoing a similar sentiment [Nad13]:

> Years ago books mattered more in provoking change. It is up to readers today not to be overwhelmed by information overload, to be selective and make books matter again.

Now I love Ralph Nader and Noam Chomsky and Thomas Piketty and Bernie Sanders and Sasha Abramsky. In fact, this section really isn't about Thomas Piketty at all.

It's more about my friend who believes that if we can just get people the right facts, they will make better decisions.

There is tremendous value in these scholars' work advancing the science. Piketty's book may be the most important piece of research on the economy to date in the 21st century.

When it comes to politics, however, people don't suddenly slap themselves on the forehead and say "Ah, I've been wrong all along. Given this new information, I will suddenly 'compute' a better response."

Recent science has actually demonstrated that often, in fact, the opposite is true. Presented with information that contradicts a core belief, people may aggressively defend this belief [Moon12].

Using data and scientific arguments works when you're talking to people in certain settings, academic settings. However, when it comes to politics, while you might be able to persuade some people, science itself suggests that this is not the most effective approach.

To understand why, it helps to look at another metaphor for the mind derived from more recent science.

1.6 Reframing the mind as an associative network

Recent research into the mind and discoveries in the field of artificial neural networks suggest that the metaphor of the mind as a computer is just as flawed as the metaphor of the mind as a steam engine.

From medical research, we know our brain consists of millions of biological neurons. How do these neurons function together to produce thought? How do these neurons work together as a single unit, the human brain?

The field of artificial neural networks offers some insights into how these millions of neurons turn input into decisions. While still a relatively new science, it's important (and fairly easy) to understand this model metaphorically because of the implications for politics.

Figure 1.7 shows a simple artificial neural network, a back propagation network, consisting of an input layer (sensors), any number of hidden layers (where the "thinking" occurs through the weighted connections w_{ij} and w_{jk}), and an output layer (representing the decision) [Gal93].

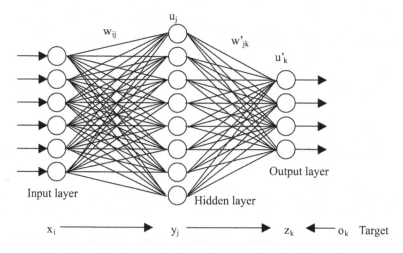

Figure 1.7   Conceptual diagram of an artificial neural network. [Gal13]

Artificial neural networks (ANNs), like the above, contain a learning rule, which modifies the weights of the connections according to the input and desired recognition of that input.

During this "learning" or training algorithm, information is stored in the weights and connections that allows the network to respond to a given set of inputs.

Here is a quick example:

> You want to train an ANN to recognize the number 5. You present it with a series of numbers over and over again while you're training the neural network. Each time a number is presented, the network makes a guess whether it is a 5 or not. You provide the network with positive or negative (right or wrong) feedback about its guess and this feedback is used to adjust the levels in the hidden layer of neurons.

In this manner, the ANN "learns" to recognize the number 5 (or another number or image that the ANN has been trained to recognize).

One of the important things to note for ANNs is that you typically have to expose them to thousands of training runs with feedback before the hidden layer weights adjust. Simulated on a computer, depending on the complexity of the ANN, this can take a bit of time.

Don't worry right now if you don't understand exactly how this works. It's more important when it comes to politics to think about an associative network of neurons as a better metaphor for the mind than a computer.

1.7 Implications

In an artificial neural network model of the human brain, information is stored in the connections.

Rather than a model where data flows from memory to a CPU for computation, neurons act as both computer and memory. As a neuron processes an input, it modifies connections. The brain does not have a separate processing unit and separate memory unit.

Similarly, it is believed something similar happens in the human brain though there is still much about the human brain we do not know. A way to conceptualize this, however, is that connections are shaped as we experience and try different things and subsequently receive feedback.

Our memory is associative rather than accessible by a specific computer address. We are able to "request" information from our brain and our brain is often able to "retrieve" it. Just not with the unerring preciseness of computer memory. Barring equipment failure or memory degeneration, computer memory is virtually infallible. Given a specific address, a computer will return the appropriate 1 or 0 every time. Our own memory system functions much differently as evidenced by how we often struggle to recall a specific piece of information.

The associative connections of our minds, orders of magnitude more complex than within any ANN, allow us to think and make decisions.

One way to think about these connections and associations is as a frame, a series of connections, that we use to reason in a particular instance.

For example, if you want to purchase shoes, you use the series of connections, or frame, associated with a shoe. A shoe is a piece of clothing for human feet. Shoes have soles, arches, heels and may be buckled, laced on, or fastened on with Velcro. Shoes also have various attributes that help ensure you choose a proper shoe. Size, color, type, purpose, cost, and so on. You likely learned how to conceptualize shoes from your parents growing up.

This conceptual frame changes and evolves as you learn more about shoes. For instance, when I took up running, I learned about stability in a running shoe after getting shin splints. I asked other runners and went to a specialized running store to find shoes that wouldn't give me shin splints and they explained that some running shoes have more stability than others.

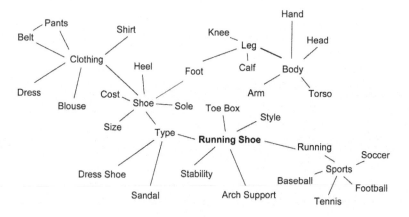

Figure 1.8   Some of the associations for "running shoe."

Even though they're all just various forms of foot clothing, I used new experiences and feedback to add to my conceptual frame about shoes.

Similarly, as evidenced from some of the examples about the mind, our frames about how we think have evolved over time.

If you believe, for example, that the human mind is a hydraulic system using four basic humors and that an excess of one of these humors causes disease, it might make sense to bleed a person to try to restore a balance of humors. If, however, you believe the human mind is a computer or a neural network, bleeding someone to try to cure melancholia sounds absurd.

Is this how the mind works?

Not exactly. Remember, we're talking about metaphors and how we conceptualize our own thinking.

An associative network is a better metaphor for the mind, a better way to think about thinking, than a computer. We still don't know exactly how the mind works. An artificial neural network does not model or duplicate the human mind.

From what we know to date, computers don't make the best metaphors for the mind. ANNs are a better metaphor.

I also use this example to show how behavior often changes only when conceptual frames change.

To quote George Lakoff [Lak06]:

> When the facts don't fit the frame, the frame stays and the facts are ignored.

1.8 Conceptual frames and computer programs

A computer program is a one-time piece of code that gets written and translated by a central processor and does one thing exactly the same every time.

In the mind as a computer metaphor, programming means to write a specific piece of code, input it to the "computer mind," and the mind will act according to the program.

It's easy to think of information as a computer program. That is, it's easy to assume that if you input the the right information about income inequality, for example, that people will compute the right result and solution for income inequality.

We often envision people "processing" information or data and producing a very specific output each time similar to a computer. A computer won't spit out a different result given the same set of information in the same circumstances. A computer program will always produce the same output (at least deterministic algorithms anyways).

If you are a programmer, this concept is very helpful when it comes to fixing bugs. If something was working correctly and suddenly it's not working right anymore, the first question is always, what did you (or someone else) change in the code?

If our minds work more like neural networks, our minds adjust chemical levels (or weights) in our biological neurons over time according to our experiences and feedback. This is why good academic programs accommodate different learning styles and provide opportunities for practice and experience, such as labs or practicums.

Over time and with enough practice we learn through feedback to react to different scenarios and situations.

This is one way to think of a conceptual frame—as literally a series of associations (or neural weights) in our mind that we both use and adjust every time we respond to a situation.

When I talk to people about Lakoff's work, invariably people relate it to language: we just need to use the right language.

In a sense yes, it is about language, but it's not about simply finding the right language.

The way I've seen people interpret framing is that they just need to come up with the right terms. We just need to replace 'liberal' with 'progressive,' for example. Or, instead of saying 'tax relief,' we should say 'freeloading.'

For language to work, however, the appropriate conceptual frame has to exist. Assuming we need to use the right language ignores the process of building conceptual frames in order for the use of language to even matter. In a different day and age, this process would have been called teaching.

Lakoff says it best [Lak04]:

> Reframing is not just about words and language. Reframing is about ideas. The ideas have to be in place in people's brains before the sound bite can make any sense.

In other words, sometimes when you're speaking with someone and you think that the person just doesn't "seem to get it," it's literally because the person is reasoning from a completely different conceptual frame.

It's not that someone's computer mind isn't processing the information correctly. A better way to view the challenge is that people have learned a different conceptual frame; they've learned to respond differently to similar information.

We often characterize a person's behavior as "stupid" because in our metaphorical conception of the mind, if someone doesn't compute a similar answer given the same set of data, our own values and beliefs tell us that the person's computer mind must be broken. The person is not running the program correctly.

So what do we typically do?

We keep feeding in the same data hoping for a different conclusion and are constantly surprised when we don't see one. We grow frustrated and get angry.

When facts don't fit the frame and someone continues using the frame, our gut reaction is to label the person as "stupid."

Yet when facts about the human mind don't fit our frame of the human mind, we discard these facts and continue to do what *we've* been doing ineffectually for years.

Does this make us "stupid"?

> In its ideas about itself as in all of its other endeavors, the mind goes from mastery to enslavement. By an irresistible movement, which imitates the attraction death exercises over life, thought again and again uses the instruments of its own freedom to bind itself in chains.
> –Roberto Unger [Ung75]

1.9   Common beliefs when it comes to politics

Here are a few of the political beliefs I've observed that may well have their roots in rationalism or the "mind as a computer" frame:

- "The truth will set you free." This is the belief that simply exposing someone to the right set of facts will convince them of the error of their ways.

- Voters vote on issues. Plug in an issue that people support, and voters will vote based on this issue.

- Framing is simply choosing the right language; this belief assumes the pre-existence of similar conceptual frames of understanding.

- People should naturally "compute" the same response to the same facts. If they don't after a single instance their "computer mind" is somehow broken or "stupid."

- The more facts, the better. Previously, I quoted Ralph Nader talking about information overload. Isn't part of this information overload due to the fact that we keep trying to publish the single book of facts that's going to change everything? (And yes, I understand irony. I think we have enough information to take action. I think people by and large know we live in an oligarchy. The question is, what to do about it?)

If your conceptual frame for the human mind is a computer, it's very easy to believe that people should draw similar conclusions from the same set of data or facts. The key in this situation is simply getting people the right input.

If, however, you conceptualize the mind as a neural network where people make decisions based on conceptual frames and metaphors they've learned over the years, you start to see why you might not win people over with facts. Especially if they've established different conceptual models and are viewing the facts through a different lens.

A great example is income inequality. If you believe "free markets" always lead to a greater good, you're likely to believe the solution to income inequality is more deregulation and less government involvement. If you believe in democracy and mutual responsibility, you're likely to believe that those who benefit more should return more.

Don't get me wrong, facts are critical. Science and facts are at the heart of our best conceptual frames.

For example, it would be difficult if not impossible to conceptualize the mind as a neural network if scientists hadn't conducted research into mathematical models for human neurons and brain functions.

If I hadn't been exposed to the science of artificial neural networks, I would quite likely still think of the mind as a computer, simply because I wouldn't have any conception how billions of biological neurons interact together to form thought.

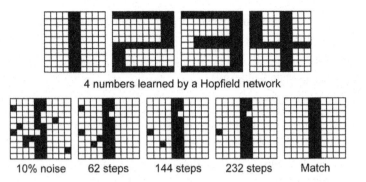

4 numbers learned by a Hopfield network

| 10% noise | 62 steps | 144 steps | 232 steps | Match |

Figure 1.9   Simulated Hopfield network recognizing the number "1".

Conceptual frames, however, go beyond science. They require new language, visualizations, culture, examples, and teachers. To this day, for example, I still remember the power of programming a Hopfield network on a computer, running a training algorithm on it to adjust the internal weights so it would recognize numbers, and then watching as it correctly identified numbers.

I would never have learned about artificial neural networks without college, without a teacher who had studied for years before me, without scientists who had conducted the research, without the people who had written research papers and the textbook, and without doable projects and exercises.

I wasn't just given a set of facts and left on my own.

I also would never have thought about using this metaphor to rethink my approach to political discussions.

The work of Lakoff and others has led me to:

- Identify the frames others use when they speak about politics.

- Understand and explain my own beliefs and frames (because others often share them).

- Recognize framing as more than finding the right language. I like to think of framing as language, learning, and teaching.

- Focus on winning people over and teaching (rather than winning arguments).

- Recognize the importance of visuals, stories, and other methods of teaching.

- Learn to use facts to help build or draw out different frames (rather than as an end all/be all).

- Be more patient.

- Repeat myself in different ways (building or reinforcing conceptual frames takes time and repetition).

- Provide feedback (especially positive feedback when you agree with someone).

The following chapters go into much more detail, but before beginning I felt it critical to illustrate the importance of conceptual frames (such as the mind as a computer) to how we behave and think about politics.

> If you start with networks, you think very differently about politics.
> — Drew Westen, *The Political Brain*. [Wes07]

1.10 Emotion

How does a neural network frame for the mind take emotion into account?

To the best of my knowledge, though there are several theories, science isn't yet able to completely explain emotion.

If you think of our minds as having evolved over thousands of years, the mind can be viewed as layers of neural networks with areas of the brain like the prefrontal cortex (responsible for higher-level reasoning) and older, more primitive areas of the brain, such as the limbic system (responsible for emotion).

Chris Mooney conceptualizes this as **System 1** ("the emotional brain") and **System 2** ("the reasoning brain") [Moon12].

System 1 governs our rapid fire "fight or flight" emotional responses while System 2 is responsible for our slower, more conscious cognitive processes.

System 2's operations, however, are not free from emotional bias and, in many circumstances, System 1's emotional response may drive the direction of System 2.

In 2006, Drew Westen conducted one of the first scientific experiments on emotion in politics. Westen used Magnetic Resonance Imaging (MRI) to

The Limbic System

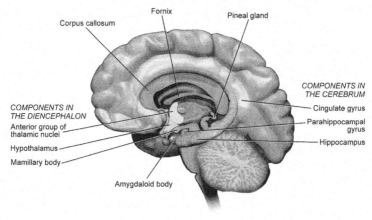

Figure 1.10 Components of the limbic system. [Bla14]

look at the areas of the brain activated when self-described Democrats or Republicans heard contradictory remarks about their favored political candidate [Wes06].

The experiment:

- Recruit 30 men, 50% committed Democrats, 50% committed Republicans.

- Put the recruits under an MRI machine and show them quotes where a political candidate reversed a position.

- Quotes were by George W. Bush and John Kerry.

- Everyone was shown all of the quotes and also neutral quotes by a neutral person (Tom Hanks).

Republicans judged John Kerry harshly and let George W. Bush off the hook. Democrats judged George W. Bush harshly and let John Kerry slide.

The areas of the brain responsible for reasoning showed little activity while drawing these conclusions. The areas of the brain controlling emotions showed increased activity as compared to the subject's responses to politically neutral statements.

After partisans had ignored rational information and come to completely biased conclusions not only did negative emotion circuits (disgust, sadness, and so on) turn off, but areas of the brain involved in reward were triggered.

In other words, partisans responded in many ways as if they personally were being attacked and were rewarded when they defended their group.

Westen writes:

> None of the circuits involved in conscious reasoning were particularly engaged. Essentially, it appears as if partisans twirl the cognitive kaleidoscope until they get the conclusions they want, and then they get massively reinforced for it, with the elimination of negative emotional states and activation of positive ones.

Westen's research shows that when facts are viewed as an attack on the individual (or group), individuals respond by rationalizing the behavior of the group member and judging the behavior of the non-group member. Our System 1 brain takes over and drives System 2.

The research suggests that we are unlikely to win partisans over to a particular viewpoint they don't already hold by showing them contradictory facts.

Brendan Nyhan and Jason Reifler have also conducted research into whether misperceptions can be corrected [Nyh10]. In several studies, they have actually found evidence of a "backfire effect" in which refutations actually *increase* the emotional misperception.

The first experiment they conducted showed participants fake newspaper articles where the claim that that Saddam Hussein possessed weapons of mass destruction was first suggested (in a real-life 2004 quote):

> There was a risk, a real risk, that Saddam Hussein would pass weapons or materials or information to terrorist networks, and in the world after September the 11th, that was a risk we could not afford to take.
> George W. Bush, 2005.

And then refuted (with a discussion of the findings of the 2004 CIA Duelfer report):

> In 2004, the Central Intelligence Agency released a report that concludes that Saddam Hussein did not possess stockpiles of illicit weapons at the time of the U.S. invasion in March 2003, nor was any program to produce them under way at the time.

What they found from the experiment was that not only were factual corrections unlikely to change minds, but in the most ideological, they even had the effect of strengthening the false belief.

Similar results occurred when conservatives were confronted with factual evidence refuting the claim that the Bush tax cuts increased government revenue. After the correction, core conservatives believed the false claim more strongly.

Recently, Nyhan and Reifler conducted an experiment testing strategies to communicate the factual importance of vaccinations [Moon14]. A representative sample of 1,759 Americans with at least one child at home was used.

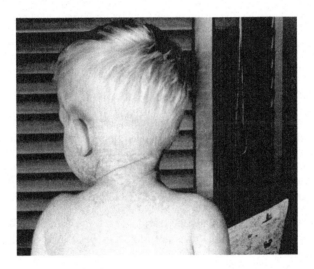

Figure 1.11   Child with measles in the 1960s. [CDC63]

Several of the messages/images tested provoked a similar backfire effect among vaccine deniers. The least effective messages, "Disease narrative" and "Disease images," increased respondents' likelihood that the vaccines themselves would cause disease from 7.7% to 13.8%. Digging into the data, they found that the increase occurred because of a strong backfire effect among the minority who were most distrustful of vaccines.

Nyhan highlights the takeaway:

> I don't think our results imply that they shouldn't communicate why vaccines are a good idea. But they do suggest that we should be more careful

to test the messages that we use, and to question the intuition that countering misinformation is likely to be the most effective strategy.

1.11 Coda

At some point in this chapter, you probably said to yourself: "Wait a second, I see what you're doing. You're trying to demonstrate the importance of framing by reframing how we think about thinking."

If you did, you are correct. I wanted to demonstrate the importance of framing and also lay the groundwork for the more practical chapters.

A quick recap:

1. Conceptual frames for the human mind have changed over time.

2. The mind doesn't work the way we think it does.

3. The mind as a computer is the metaphor that underlies some of our basic assumptions about politics (and many other things as well).

4. An associative network is a better conceptual frame for the mind. We think in an associative manner, more like artificial neural networks than computers, using frames and metaphors.

5. If we want to help someone learn a new frame, we need to challenge existing frames and use appropriate language and visualizations to teach the new frame.

6. It's quite likely that we'll need to repeat this framing.

Hopefully, discussing framing self-consciously in this fashion helps to illustrate how we learn and process information using conceptual frames and how these frames both help us and hinder us in ways we often don't recognize.

When science tells us that facts don't win people over when it comes to beliefs, do we a) continue with the same ineffectual arguments that often make us so angry, or b) change?

If you already know this, you're ahead of the game. If you're starting to think that our tactics need to change, then I've demonstrated it can be done. Not only that but it's not as hard as you might think.

PRACTICE

1.1 "Mind like a steel trap" is an example of a metaphor (technically a simile in this instance) for the human mind. What other metaphors can you think of that are used to describe the human mind?

1.2 When you conceptualize how you "think," what does your model look like? What elements does it contain? How do the different elements work together to do things like find information or solve a problem?

1.3 Do you talk to people about politics? What do your conversations sound like? What do other conversations you hear sound like?

1.4 Think of someone you know who you find stubborn or religious about a particular subject. How would you describe this person's beliefs? Does this person know about his or her beliefs? (Often it's easier to see these conceptual frames in others than it is to see them in ourselves.)

CHAPTER 2

THE DIRECTION OF CHANGE

All along the watchtower, princes kept the view
While all the women came and went, barefoot servants, too.
Outside in the distance a wildcat did growl.
Two riders were approaching, the wind began to howl.
                                                    —Bob Dylan, 1967. [Dyl67]

There are many ways to look at how the United States has changed over time.

I'm going to do this by following a single issue. The issue is tax policy and I'm choosing this issue because it's the number one issue for the number one lobbying group in our country—the U.S. Chamber of Commerce.

The Chamber's Economic and Tax Policy division describes their goal as follows [CoC14]:

> Our division is committed to pro-growth tax policies that preserve America's global competitiveness and is opposed to tax increases that reduce businesses' ability to grow, invest, and create jobs.

For the purpose of drawing a picture about the direction of change, I'm going to use this chart (Table 2.1) when talking about taxes:

	Receives most of the benefit	
Type of tax reduction	**The 1%**	**Everyone Else**
Income tax (>$400K)	X	
Income tax (<$400K)		X
Capital gains tax	X	
Sales tax		X
Luxury tax	X	
FICA (Social Security) payroll tax		X
Corporate tax	X	
Estate tax	X	
Local property tax		X

Table 2.1   Who benefits most from tax reductions.

Let's look at how the Chamber of Commerce has fared over the past 40 years when it comes to tax changes that benefit corporations. Keep in mind this exercise is meant to demonstrate a general trend rather than to chart the complete history of tax code policy.

In 1978, the Carter administration reduced the top tax rate on capital gains to 28% from 39%, reduced income taxes, increased the capital gains exclusion rate from 50% to 60%, and reduced the corporate tax rate from 48% to 46% [Mci96].

Capital gains are profits made from selling things like a house or more commonly, stocks and bonds. Subsequently, the capital gains tax is not a tax that most people pay; this tax primarily affects the people who make their living from capital. Most people earn a living from income from their labor.

At the onset of income taxes, capital gains were taxed at the same rate as other income, up to 77% during World War I. In 1981, Reagan cut the capital gains tax even further, to 20%, the lowest rate since Herbert Hoover. In other words, people who sell stocks and bonds often pay much less than people who earn a living from their labor.

In 1981, Reagan passed the Economic Recovery Tax Act (ERTA). This included:

- Across-the-board income tax cuts. The top income tax rate dropped from 70% to 50%; the bottom rate dropped from 14% to 11%.

- Raising the estate tax exemption to $600,000.

These cuts were based on the idea that we could cut taxes and increase revenue through greater growth. Unfortunately, so much revenue was lost that Congress had to repeal several of these tax cuts only a year later with the Tax Equity and Fiscal Responsibility Act (TEFRA) of 1982.

What we don't often hear is that Social Security taxes were raised five times from 1977 to 1990. Social security taxes are the biggest tax paid by ordinary people, according to Reagan himself [Rea81]:

> For the nation's work force, the Social Security tax is already the biggest tax they pay. In 1935 we were told the tax would never be greater than 2% of the first $3,000 of earnings. It is presently 13.3% of the first $29,700, and the scheduled increases will take it to 15.3% of the first $60,600.

These tax increases on workers subsidized tax cuts for corporations and the wealthy, like the capital gains tax cuts and the estate tax cut. The direction of tax cut changes lurched heavily in favor of the U.S. Chamber of Commerce during Reagan's administration.

In 1986, in the second of his two major tax overhauls, the top tax rate for individuals was reduced from 50% to 28%, while the bottom rate was raised from 11% to 15%.

Our country was sold on this idea with the philosophy that giving money to corporations and wealthy investors would create a "trickle down effect" in which everyone would benefit. This was also popularized through sayings like: "a rising tide lifts all boats."

As a result of the trickle down tax cuts of the 1980s, revenue fell and the deficit rose. That led the first President Bush to raise taxes in 1990 to try to keep the deficit in check. For this reason, I draw the direction away from the U.S. Chamber of Commerce from 1988-1992.

In 1993, President Clinton raised the top two income tax rates slightly and raised the corporate tax rate 1% (from 34% to 35%). However, he also increased the share of Social Security benefits that could be taxed and raised the sales tax on fuel (a consumption tax that affects consumers more than businesses). The direction during Clinton's first term was mostly flat.

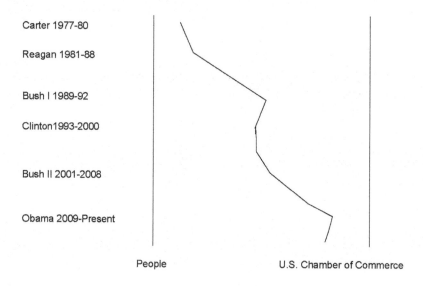

Figure 2.1 Ideological direction of tax policy since 1976.

In 1997, however, Clinton reduced the capital gains tax from 28% to 20% and raised the exemption on the estate tax to $1 million from $600,000. Here, the direction moves in the direction of the Chamber.

Note: If we were talking about trade or global finance, the direction of change shifted even more in favor of the Chamber during Clinton's term with the passage of NAFTA and the repeal of the Glass-Steagall Act. Though I'm graphing tax policy, I think many people forget how much the Chamber of Commerce accomplished under President Clinton.

George W. Bush accelerated the push in 2001 and 2003 with more tax cuts heavily favoring the wealthy. The exemption for the estate tax was raised to $5 million and the rate reduced. The Center on Budget and Policy Priorities estimates that 24.2% of tax savings from these changes went to the top 1% [Fri04].

In 2010, the Bush tax cuts were up for renewal. President Obama fought to renew them for those earning less than $200,000 ($250,000 for joint filers). The U.S. Chamber vigorously fought leaving out those who earned more and eventually a compromise was reached where the original changes were extended for 2 years in exchange for some economic stimulus measures and a temporary 1-year reduction in the payroll tax. Largely, little changed during the first Obama term.

In 2012, the Bush tax cuts came up again. This time President Obama proposed making the tax cuts permanent for those with taxable incomes of $400,000 ($450,000 for joint filers) or less. For those above this level, the rate was increased from 35% to 39.6% and the capital gains tax was also raised from 15% to 20%. The payroll tax deduction from 2010 was eliminated.

Now we could dispute the details of Figure 2.1 all day. Does it move more or less under a certain president? Are there other points to consider?

Regardless, I think we would still likely agree that the overall direction would be the same. Overall, corporate special interest groups have been successful in shifting tax policy in their favor.

Figure 2.2 illustrates the sources of revenue for the United States government (by percentage) since 1950.

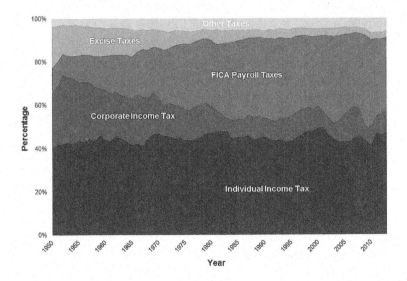

Figure 2.2   Sources of revenue for the U.S. government from 1950-2013 [Bud14].

In 1952, corporate income taxes provided 32.1% of federal revenue. By 2013, corporate income taxes provided only 9.9%. In 1952, FICA payroll taxes provided 9.7% of federal revenue. In 2013, FICA payroll taxes provided 34.2%. Excise taxes including the estate tax provided 19.1% of federal revenue in 1952. By 2013, excise taxes provided only 5.5% of federal revenue [Bud14].

	1952	**2013**	**% Change**
Corporate Income Tax	32.1%	9.9%	-22.2%
FICA Payroll Tax	9.7%	34.2%	+24.5%
Excise Taxes (Including Estate Tax)	19.1%	5.5%	-16.7%

Table 2.2   Percent changes in government revenue 1952-2013. [Bud14]

At the national level, the Chamber fights vigorously for income tax, corporate tax, estate tax, and capital gains tax reductions. Not surprisingly, these tax changes tend to do very well. The Chamber cares very little about lowering sales taxes or payroll taxes or property taxes or income taxes for those earning less than $400,000. Correspondingly, these taxes are often stealthily raised to make up for gaps in revenue.

The Chamber has been hugely successful with their campaign to make and keep the tax code exceedingly friendly to those at the top of the income scale. The net effect is a shifting of who pays.

This may be because the Chamber receives most of their funding from a few corporations. In 2009, for example, 16 companies provided 55% of their total budget [Mck11]. In other words, they don't speak for all businesses, they speak for a few very well-heeled businesses interested in short-term gains.

One of the interesting things about this chart is that the general direction is always in favor of the U.S. Chamber of Commerce. There are slight differences here and there but whether there's a Republican or Democrat in the White House seems to make little difference.

2.1   The Overton Window

How do they do it?

How did the U.S. Chamber of Commerce and other corporate special interest groups take an extremely unpopular issue (tax cuts for the wealthy) and manage to shift the landscape so radically in their favor since 1976?

Conservative think tank strategy makes heavy use of a concept called the Overton Window [Atk06]. You can also think of this as shifting the center.

The steps a policy idea takes to full legitimacy are roughly as follows:

1. Unthinkable

2. Radical

3. Acceptable

4. Sensible

5. Popular

6. Policy

Joseph Overton, a former vice president of the Mackinac Center for Public Policy developed a way of visualizing an idea in terms of progress.

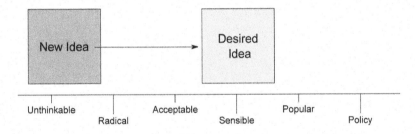

Figure 2.3   Steps in turning an idea into public policy.

Overton also realized that ideas could be made more acceptable and sensible by introducing even more radical ideas. Figure 2.3 shows how introducing a new idea can shift the desired idea closer towards realizable policy.

If you want to make conceal and carry permits look reasonable, for example, you could introduce the idea that anyone should be able to carry a firearm at any time. By comparison, conceal and carry laws look more sensible.

Overton also theorized that ideas could be placed on a spectrum from government solutions to non-government solutions. The Mackinac Center views all solutions on this spectrum and works to constantly shift the range of acceptable solutions towards their desired goal of privatization.

Within this spectrum, the Overton Window is the range of actual, reasonable possibilities as perceived by the general public. Any ideas outside of the Overton Window are radical or unthinkable.

Figure 2.4 illustrates the Overton Window for education as found on the Mackinac Center's website.

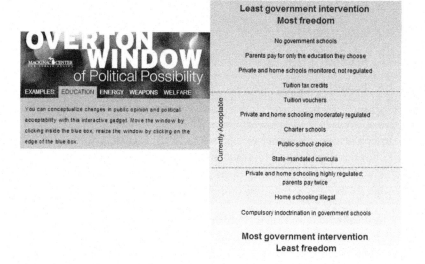

Figure 2.4   Mackinac Center Overton Window for education. [Mac14]

Ideas shown within the "Currently Acceptable" window are considered politically possible by today's Washington establishment. This is the Overton Window of acceptable solutions. Anything outside of this window is considered not politically possible and/or radical.

The idea is to gradually shift this window closer and closer to eliminating public education. Charter schools are not the end goal, the end goal is the elimination of public schools. However, this is considered radical in today's environment so ideas like charter schools and school "choice" are introduced as stepping stones to move away from public schools. The complete elimination of public schools is used to make these steps seem acceptable and sensible.

At any moment in time certain solutions are considered reasonable because of the values people hold. If you can shift the values, you shift the center, and you shift the window of acceptable solutions.

In the case of education and many other areas of public policy, freedom has been redefined as "consumer choice" and is used to shift the center away from what used to be one of our most valued institutions: our public schools.

In the past, for example, public schools were viewed as providing an equal opportunity for all and were considered one of the reasons for the success of our country. Public schools were viewed as much more as "popular" and "sensible" by the general public than they are today.

Today, corporate special interest groups have shifted values so far in an individualistic, laissez-faire market direction, that our public school system, once thought of as increasing access to education for millions of people, can be characterized as "compulsory indoctrination in government schools."

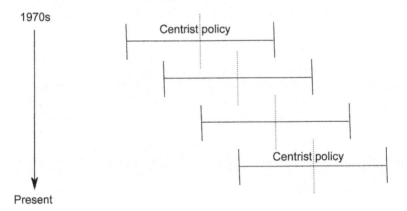

Figure 2.5   Shifting the center.

If people think only within this conceptual frame of "more consumer choice" vs. "big, bad government" established by corporate special interest groups, then privatizing education starts to look reasonable.

Shifting values not only provides political cover for the politicians implementing solutions, but allows politicians with ever more corporate views to become electable.

Today, for example, the policies of Ronald Reagan would be considered moderate or center right.

If values can be shifted ever further in a pro-corporate direction, more corporate ideas become possible and populist ideas become more radical.

We've seen this happen with our tax system. Luxury taxes that once made sense to us as a nation, such as the estate tax, are now viewed by many as an attack on individual freedom.

The primary values promoted by corporate think tanks include:

- Free markets: Markets are natural and don't require any rules.
- Individualism and selfishness.
- Personal responsibility.
- Smaller government.

Because most people know the frames for these values so well, I'm not going to talk about them here.

In many ways, we all hold some of these values. For example, we all tend to believe that personal responsibility is a good thing. And we'd likely agree that in many instances it's OK to be selfish.

The issue, rather, is the extreme manner in which groups like the Chamber promote these values to shift the Overton Window in order to pass ever more favorable policies. Also, organizations like the Chamber increase their own power when they diminish government. So they promote extreme views like "markets always regulate themselves" and "government is the problem" in order to further their agenda.

Rather than look at scientific and economic research for ideas, corporate special interest groups start with the policies they want to promote (shifting "who pays" in our country, for example) and then search for conceptualizations and methods to make these policies possible. They find fringe ideas like those of Ayn Rand and Austrian economists and use these extremes to shift the center ever further in a corporate direction.

Typically, we fight against these tactics in a defensive fashion by disputing the facts. What we don't do a good job of is providing better conceptual frames within which to think about the issues.

As long as we fight within the defined corporate special interest frames, we will continue to lose. Who wouldnt choose "freedom" over "big government" given the corporate framing?

This is why values like "freedom" and how we frame the spectrum of choices are so incredibly important.

By comparison, another way to think about freedom (and how we used to think about freedom) is as education and opportunity. Education is probably the single greatest factor in determining economic success and subsequent freedom in our society.

Using this definition of freedom, it's not hard to reframe educational policy options along a different conceptual spectrum, from least opportunity to most opportunity and freedom for everyone.

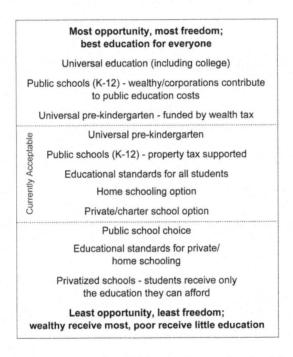

Figure 2.6   The Overton Window for a better educational frame.

If we believe better and increased opportunities lead to greater freedom, it's much easier to make the case for public education. This becomes possible if we win the fight over the definition of freedom.

It doesn't become possible by calling people stupid. It doesn't become possible by trying to compare public schools to private schools. It doesn't become possible by disputing private schools with research.

It becomes possible by framing freedom as equal opportunity for everyone. Freedom is much more than consumer choice, it's about the ability of people to pursue their goals and dreams. Equal opportunity in education makes this possible for everyone.

Another way to advance the cause of public education is to continue to introduce new ideas that increase opportunity. A few examples of this are universal pre-kindergarten and the idea of free college for everyone.

If we want to see more progress on tactical policies, we should be focusing on the more strategic fight for our nation's values. If we continue to fight within the conceptual windows defined by corporate think tanks, we will continue to lose.

2.2   The Powell Memo

We don't have much insight into the operations of the Chamber, but one fantastic early source that highlights much of their strategy is the Powell Memo.

During the 1960s, U.S. corporations felt threatened by populist movements.

In 1971, Lewis Powell, fearing that values he held dear were under attack, wrote a memo to the U.S. Chamber of Congress [Pow71] containing a detailed list of suggestions for the future direction of the Chamber. His advice centered on how corporations needed to organize and aggressively fight against democracy.

On campuses across the country, Powell wrote that the U.S. Chamber of Commerce should:

- Establish a staff of highly qualified scholars and speakers who believe in the system.
- Establish a speakers bureau of executives from "the top echelons of American business."
- Evaluate social science textbooks and "balance" with pro-business views.
- Demand equal time on the campus.
- Insert pro-business faculty on college campuses.
- Tailor similar programs for secondary education.

In terms of communications with the public, Powell suggested businesses:

51/167 4cc 8/23/71

CONFIDENTIAL MEMORANDUM

ATTACK ON AMERICAN FREE ENTERPRISE SYSTEM

TO: Mr. Eugene B. Sydnor, Jr.   DATE: August 23, 1971
           Chairman
           Education Committee
           U.S. Chamber of Commerce

FROM: Lewis F. Powell, Jr.

This memorandum is submitted at your request as a
basis for the discussion on August 24 with Mr. Booth and others
at the U.S. Chamber of Commerce. The purpose is to identify the
problem, and suggest possible avenues of action for further
consideration.

Figure 2.7   Opening of the Powell Memo to the U.S. Chamber of Commerce.
[Pow71]

- Monitor television, radio, and the press in the same manner as textbooks.

- Demand equal time.

- Publish in academic journals.

- Publish pro-business paperbacks and pamphlets.

- Purchase advertising to inform and enlighten the American people.

Here are a few other Powell suggestions on how the U.S. Chamber of Commerce should act when it comes to the political arena:

- "Political power is necessary; that such power must be assiduously cultivated; and that when necessary, it must be used aggressively and with determination."

- "The judiciary may be the most important instrument for social, economic, and political change."

- "There should be no hesitation to attack the Naders, the Marcuses, and others who openly seek destruction of the system. There should not be the slightest hesitation to press vigorously in all political arenas for support of the enterprise system. Nor should there be reluctance to penalize politically those who oppose it."

The primary goal of the strategies within the Powell Memo was shifting American values in a pro-corporate, pro-Chamber direction. The Chamber created a values-based movement.

2.3   The signal and the noise

Signal-to-noise ratio (SNR) is a measurement used in communications to compare the level of desired signal to the level of background noise.

In analog communications, such as AM/FM radio or analog television broadcasts, a high SNR ratio means that you will receive a signal with little static or interference.

To enable effective communication, you want to maximize your SNR ratio—more signal, less noise.

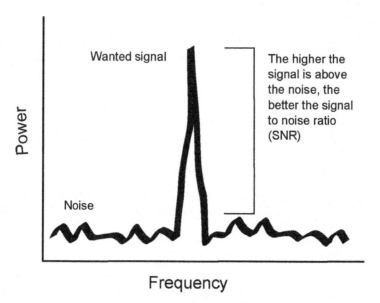

Figure 2.8   Signal to Noise Ratio.

This concept is useful in examining corporate strategies for communicating in today's media environment.

2.3.1   The signal: Values

I've often heard Fox News referred to as "Fox Noise" or "Faux Noise". From a communications standpoint, this is a flawed analogy. Fox News is the signal. Along with the other corporate media in print, TV, or radio.

Fox News, ClearChannel radio shows like *The Rush Limbaugh Show*, and conservative print and online outlets such as *The Washington Times* and *Newsmax* broadcast the core of the corporate values message.

They evangelize and promote certain values with the goal of moving the policy goal posts. They work to win people over to their worldview to make previously undesirable solutions acceptable (or even desirable).

They focus on building and maintaining a values-based coalition first and political action second.

2.4   The noise: Divide and conquer strategies

But this and this alone doesn't produce a singularly clear signal. To produce a clearer signal, corporate special interest groups have designed several strategies to disrupt other messages. Most of these strategies are some variation of the divide-and-conquer strategy.

2.4.1   Left vs. right

The first divide-and-conquer strategy is the culture war we're all familiar with: left vs. right.

This strategy is useful in a couple of situations. First, left vs. right is a much more favorable split for corporations than people vs. corporations. This was the split that started to emerge during the 1960s that the U.S. Chamber of Commerce feared most.

The biggest fear—and you can hear it clearly in the Powell Memo—is that people will get together and vote in their common interest. That is, their biggest fear is democracy. Society should be governed by and for the business class and democracy is viewed as a competitive threat.

A good example here is the oil and gas industry. In the long-term interests of our country, it makes sense to be investing in clean energy technologies that both free us from our dependency on foreign oil and create technologies we'll need when our finite supply of fossil fuels runs out. However, certain corporations can make much more money in the short term by fighting against this shift.

From a political perspective, if the split is the long-term interests of the people of our country vs. the short-term interests of a few corporations, the people win. If this problem can be politicized and turned into Republicans vs. Democrats, our country is divided 50/50. All you have to do is pit the two sides against each other and achieve deadlock. Or, even more effectively, get them to fight over something else that has nothing to do with business interests, like abortion.

Other issues where this has happened include: health care, tax policy, and the social safety net.

The Republicans vs. Democrats divide also comes in handy when science conflicts with certain corporate goals. Climate change is one example. Turn it into a Republicans vs. Democrats fight instead of science vs. a few corporations who stand to make enormous short-term profits.

Tax cuts are another example. When data and economics tell us that it's impossible to lower taxes and increase revenue, simply turn it into a Republicans vs. Democrats fight. The false divide of Republicans vs. Democrats has worked wonders for all kinds of issues.

2.4.2 Another conservative says something crazy

The second strategy I'll call liberal baiting.

Ann Coulter outlines this strategy in *How to Talk to a Liberal (If You Must)* [Cou04]:

> You must outrage the enemy. If the liberal you're arguing with doesn't become speechless with sputtering, impotent rage, you're not doing it right. People don't get angry when lies are told about them; they get angry when the truth is told about them. If you are not being called outrageous by liberals, you're not being outrageous enough. Start with the maximum assertion about liberals and then push the envelope, because, as we know, their evil is incalculable.

So the craziness is calculated?

Exactly. The key word in the Coulter quote is "speechless."

The idea is to disrupt communication (and cooperation) by turning any discussion into an emotional battle featuring conservatives and liberals. The lies corporate pundits tell are designed to sidetrack arguments, provoke emotions, and create false divides.

Corporate pundits are trained how to play this game and often guests, untrained in this brand of propaganda, either respond angrily or by talking about facts instead of a making a strong moral case.

The entertainment value back-and-forth fighting becomes noise that raises emotions on both sides rather than leads to any productive collaboration.

Fortunately, in conversations you have, there are no professionally trained corporate pundits. But you may end up talking with people who have bought into the false Republican/Democrat divide.

I characterize this divide as false because if you're able to get past the emotions and find common ground, you'll almost always find that no matter who you speak with, you have more in common than you would with a member of the truly economic elite (the 1% of the 1%, the people who encourage this divide).

As an interesting aside, this tactic appears to have been adopted from Saul Alinsky's *Rules for Radicals* [Ali71]:

> Ridicule is man's most potent weapon. It is almost impossible to counterattack ridicule. Also it infuriates the opposition, who then react to your advantage.

If you Google Saul Alinsky, all of the top search results are from corporate pundit sites. Curiously enough, I had never heard of Alinsky until a conservative friend of mine told me about him.

2.4.3   Other false divides

When your arguments start from an extreme minority position (tax breaks for the wealthy, reducing wages, reducing benefits, breaking up unions, etc.), how do you effectively market your ideas and form coalitions?

From a marketing perspective, the answer is to simply change the target markets.

The key number to get to in a Democracy is 51%.

You're probably familiar with a few ways the monied interests have retargeted the market:

- White vs. minority: The most frequent segmenting here is white vs. black. By crafting a message that appeals to whites, you shift the target markets in your favor by roughly 87%/13% in the case of black/white segmenting. If you segment the market by whites vs. Latinos the segmenting is roughly 83%/17%. Overall, according to the U.S. Census bureau, whites comprise 62.6% of the population [Cen14]. Target whites.

- Straight vs. gay: The number of people who identify as LGBT is more difficult to calculate. The Williams Institute conducted a study in 2013 that found the national average to be about 3.5% [Gat13]. However, a higher percentage acknowledge having same-sex attraction without identifying as LGBT so the exact number is in dispute. Regardless, it's clear that LGBT people are in the minority. Target heterosexuals.

- Religious vs. non-religious: According to a 2008 survey, only 15% of Americans claim no religious affiliation [Kos09]. Target the religious.

If you can appeal to 85% of Christians (or 62.6% of Caucasian America or the majority of straight Americans) instead of the .01%, you stand a much better chance.

When you have a terrible product (tax cuts for the wealthy), you win by selling something different or by distracting people's attention in other ways.

2.5   Why conservatives love Bill Maher

Lakoff and framing have been around for years, you say. True, I can't argue.

Why haven't we made more progress then?

This is an excellent question. The answer, I believe, has many facets. One component though is that liberals still struggle with the idea of framing and teaching values. I see it every day with people I know and even with prominent liberals.

A great example from March 21, 2014—Bill Maher devotes a segment of his show he calls *New Rules* to the power of language [Mah14]:

> Democrats need to stop despairing about the gloomy midterm predictions, and realize there's actually a glimmer of hope, and it has to do with suicide. Let me finish. For decades now, liberals pushed the issue of assisted suicide, and it got nowhere. Then, they started to call it "aid

Figure 2.9   The "New Rules" segment of *Real Time with Bill Maher*

in dying," and its approval shot up 20 points and it's now legal in five states. That's the power of language.

While Maher makes a valid point about the importance of language, he confuses framing with spin.   Spin is the deliberate use of language or the deliberate development of a frame to mislead.   Naming an initiative designed to undercut public education the "No Child Left Behind Act" is spin.

A frame is a conceptual model that allows us to interpret and respond to events. In George Lakoff's words, frames "shape how we reason, and they even impact how we perceive and how we act." [**?**] One way to think of a frame is as a series of associations within the mind that were both constantly using and adjusting to make decisions. These frames allow us to understand the world.

Framing is when we understand and can communicate what we genuinely believe. This is more difficult than it sounds as we often use frames quite unconsciously.

If someone believes that markets are natural and always lead to a greater good, for example, its very difficult to convince this person that we should interfere with markets. If, however, we believe that markets are human creations we have control over, it seems natural to write rules for them. Two conceptual models, two different interpretations. One model, however, stands up better to our facts and experience.

If you are talking to a person who believes markets are natural and good and trying to tell them that 30 million people were uninsured so we passed legislation to fix the problem, it will seem unnatural and wrong to them until you establish that markets are things we created and can create towards different ends. This is why its important to understand and speak at the belief level.

Most conservatives, for example, believe the frames they are communicating. They aren't trying to deliberately deceive you. Unfortunately, the corporations who have built these conceptual frames typically have a specific agenda in mind. If you can frame issues within a better conceptual model, often you can reach them quite easily.

If Maher understood framing and was truly interested in winning people over, his show would be a completely different show.

First of all, it wouldn't be a comedy show.

One of my favorite quotes on political humor comes from GOP strategist Mike Murphy [Gold04]:

> Political satire doesn't have anywhere near the power you'd think it does. Most people who watch Jon Stewart's show or a Michael Moore movie have already made up their minds.

Political humor, by definition, depends on people having a similar view of the world (similar conceptual frame) as the comedian. The humor comes from pointing out the contrasts in worldview.

For example, when Maher says:

> Perhaps you noticed how everyone on the right universally decided at the exact same moment that Obama's "weakness" is what "emboldened" Putin to take Crimea. And that's not a matter of great minds thinking alike, because for that, you would need great minds.

The audience laughs and applauds because, by and large, they already agree with Maher—Republicans are not great minds.

Now to be fair, I shouldn't pick on Bill Maher. You could say a similar thing about Jon Stewart, Stephen Colbert, or any number of political comedians— their audience typically already agrees with them.

By definition, these are comedy shows. We shouldn't expect them to win anyone over. Does this mean they're not important? No. Not at all. Comedy makes us laugh, builds identity, lifts morale, and provides a much-needed release. Many Americans, especially younger Americans, also get most of their news from comedy shows. Making news entertaining is hugely valuable.

We just shouldn't expect comedy shows to win people over because political comedy requires a similar worldview in order to "get" the jokes. Comedy plays to a specific audience that already shares similar values.

Corporations, however, have developed strategies and invested in infrastructure designed to teach values and win people over.

We seem to think that this process, what used to be called "education," is somehow a dirty word.

As you might have guessed, the title of this section is a bit tongue-in-cheek. Conservatives don't typically love Bill Maher. They hate him because he makes fun of them. Corporate lobbyists, however, are OK with Bill Maher. He's not doing anything to bring people together. His audience already agrees with him.

What about comedians on the other side? Someone like Rush Limbaugh. The Rush Limbaughs of the world spend most of their time evangelizing corporate values. Poking fun at liberals is simply part of their sermon. The majority of the time they're preaching values. The Rush Limbaughs of the world are not comedians in the same sense.

Bill Maher, Stephen Colbert, Jon Stewart are political comedians/satirists, not evangelists. You don't typically hear them promoting or teaching values. Why? Because they're political comedy shows. They get people to laugh who already agree with them.

Again, this isn't a critique of political comedians. It is simply an explanation of what they are, who their audience is, and what we don't see much of in the so-called "liberal media."

2.6 What you won't find in the "liberal media"

It's rare that you find anyone in the media winning people over by voicing traditional American values.

Oprah Winfrey was one of the best I can remember. She knew herself, she knew her values, and she was fearless when it came to speaking about both.

In 2008, Oprah spoke at Stanford University's graduation as her goddaughter, Kirby Bumpus, graduated. The speech is pure Oprah: personal, anecdotal, funny, and unashamed.

A brief excerpt [Win08]:

> And after eight months, I lost that job. They said I was too emotional. I was too much. But since they didn't want to pay out the contract, they put me on a talk show in Baltimore. And the moment I sat down on that show, the moment I did, I felt like I'd come home. I realized that TV could be more than just a playground, but a platform for service, for helping other people lift their lives. And the moment I sat down, doing that talk show, it felt like breathing. It felt right. And that's where everything that followed for me began.

From this small excerpt alone, we know what Oprah believes. She believes in helping people. She believes in public service. She believes in herself and other people.

Compare this to Bill Maher:

> Being a Republican means starting with a bedrock principle, like rich people shouldn't pay taxes, or black people shouldn't vote. (audience laughter) And then, figuring out how to sell it to low-information voters, otherwise known as Americans. Did I say "don't tax rich people?" I meant "encourage the job creators" Did I say "don't let black people vote?" I meant "clamp down on voter fraud." Did I say "bring back slavery?" I meant "phase out race-based freedom quotas."

From this quick snippet, we know that Bill Maher believes:

1. Conservatives are stupid.

2. People vote incorrectly because they lack sufficient information; they are "low-information" voters. (This is the rationalist belief that if we just give people better information, they will make better decisions.)

3. Conservatives are stupid.

In other words, corporations couldn't do a better job selecting someone to reinforce the idea that liberals think conservatives are stupid if they tried. Part of their story is that liberals don't get it and will tell conservatives that they're stupid and what does Bill Maher do? He tells us that conservatives are stupid.

Remember, most corporate strategies are divide-and-conquer cultural identity strategies. Gays vs. straights. Religious vs. non-religious. White vs. minority. Men vs. women. Republicans vs. Democrats.

Bill Maher's show is a show for people who already share the same beliefs as Bill Maher and want to laugh at "dumb" conservatives.

Let's compare this to a different type of show like NBC's *All In* with Chris Hayes. The premise of *All In* is quite different. Hayes covers current news and relevant issues. Here's a quick excerpt from one of Hayes's shows about the reinstatement of a Texas abortion law [Hay13]:

> Yesterday, a federal appeals court reinstated parts of Texas's anti-abortion law that a lower court had struck down. The law, which blew up nationally during Wendy Davis's epic filibuster, means as many as 30 to 36 clinics in the state that provide abortions will have to stop doing so immediately. Yesterday's appellate court ruling means millions of women in the state of Texas will not have access to reproductive health services.

Hayes reports facts. He is outraged. He talks about the denial of service to women. The conceptual frames that link reproductive health services to freedom or the greater good of society are simply assumed

If you're a liberal reading this, you're probably thinking "Yes, obviously!"

To you and me, yes. Because you and I and Chris Hayes reason from within the same value system. We believe in mutual responsibility and a version of the economy and freedom that makes this obvious.

This is, of course, why we're outraged.

For a second, think about how you would try to explain this benefit to someone whose worldview says that everyone should act out of their own selfishness. I'll give you a hint: until you explain freedom and responsibility differently, you're going to struggle.

I enjoy Chris Hayes's show tremendously and am glad MSNBC has taken a chance on him. Nowhere on TV will you find deeper, more extensive analysis of politics. Please don't consider this an attack on Chris, or Bill, or anyone else for that matter. By definition his show is just not a show that teaches values. In media parlance, his target audience is policy wonks or those looking for a more analytical take on politics.

Rachel Maddow similarly bills her show as focusing on "the legislative proposals and policies that shape American life"—by and large, an in-depth look and analysis of current political and cultural interest stories. Lawrence O'Donnell's *The Last Word* is similar with a slightly different slant.

Values typically underlie the analysis, assumed. An easy example is the belief in rationalism. This is the belief Stephen Colbert expressed when he said:

Reality has a well-known liberal bias.

Please don't mistake me here, as this is a bit delicate. I'm a huge fan of Chris Hayes's show. Jon Stewart, Rachel Maddow, and Stephen Colbert too. Bill Maher, admittedly not so much, but that's more personal taste than anything else. I can understand why people enjoy his show.

We need news, we need policy analysis, and we need to laugh.

The problem is, corporations set the agenda and most of what's in the media is reaction. We dispute. We counter. We analyze. We joke. We call out the lies.

America receives a huge dose of corporate values through corporate media, repetition of these positions by liberal comedians or analysts, and then analysis or jokes about corporate values and positions.

This often has the undesirable effect of amplifying the message. At the very least, it's reactive.

What's strangely missing in the "liberal" media? The teachers and evangelists of the ideas on which our country was founded.

Where are the people talking about democracy and mutual responsibility and equality? Where are the people outlining a better vision for our country?

Where are the people who can teach better conceptual frames and ideas and values in a fashion that people can easily relate too?

The "liberal media" is filled with news reporters, comedians, pundits, entertainers, and policy analysts.

What you won't find in the "liberal media" are the leaders, teachers, and evangelists of American ideas and values such as democracy, mutual responsibility, and freedom.

2.7 Towards a strategy

We could speculate all day why there aren't more leaders and evangelists of the 99% in the media. Is it because this is something people don't value or is it because corporations own the media?

I don't find this particularly productive.

Our strength is in our numbers, our values, and our story. If we tell this story to the people, no amount of money or media will be able to compensate.

Do we need a strategy similar to the U.S. Chamber of Commerce?

I don't believe a similar strategy would be successful because we have different values and beliefs. For example, we don't believe in centralized hierarchical organizations.

I believe we need a different strategy, a strategy that takes advantage of our strengths. I'm going to call it a distributive strategy.

A distributive strategy assumes:

1. People vote based on values.

2. Our greatest strength is our numbers.

3. Our country was founded by people and we have a better story to tell; we have better values. (If the Chamber had decent values, it wouldn't need to spend $200 million a year on propaganda.)

4. The end goal is to win people over.

5. We're going to be at a funding disadvantage due to spending by consolidated corporate lobbying groups like the Chamber.

6. People participate when they're inspired and feel that they can make a difference.

7. People also win when they come together to achieve common goals; this is how we can beat the corporate divide-and-conquer strategies.

If we can create a million people capable of doing within their immediate circles what corporations do through their lobbying strategies and mass media, we, the people, win.

We just need to focus on some things that may feel a little uncomfortable to us at first, such as winning people over and talking about our values.

I know we have a million people willing to do this because I see them fighting every day online or in the comments sections of online newspapers. Unfortunately, they're often fighting with each other or playing some version of the liberal/conservative game.

We fight about small details on page 242 of a new policy when implementing any of the other numerous recommendations, if we could do it, would be a step in the right direction. We talk all day about how wrong some conservative pundit is when what we really need is a system for change.

If we could take this energy and put it into winning people over, it wouldn't be long before we were capable of shifting the entire landscape.

As a first step, we need to recognize that winning people over is much different than winning an argument. When you win someone over, you have a person willing to work with you towards a common goal. You don't have to agree on everything.

Joe Brewer, founder and senior researcher for *Culture2* and founder of *Cognitive Policy Works*, writes [Bre12]:

> It isn't that their ideas are better. The difference is entirely in the execution. They [corporations] set the agendas and we react to them, plain and simple.

To change this, we need to start with values. The challenge of our time is going to be building a coalition strong enough to restore democracy and the way to do this is to start with a vision of shared values.

This vision has to go beyond one person or policy issue.

We should start with a vision that sets the agenda and work towards change in the direction of our vision. We should put as much effort into our vision and how to accomplish change as we do into the specific policy changes we desire.

If we have a vision and a system for change, we could get part of it right and then work at perfecting it. We wouldn't be so afraid of having to get everything right the first time. If we had a vision and a system for change we could do things one step at a time and we wouldn't have to come up with the perfect policy to begin with.

This is why fighting for values and winning on high-level vision is so important.

When we know our values and frame them clearly, we win people over (rather than alienate them), learn to identify others who share our values, elect better representatives (who also share these values), and can collaborate more effectively on broad strategic initiatives (such as getting the money out of politics).

Fortunately, our values are strong and have a long tradition in America. We just need to get better at consciously talking about them.

2.7.1 The insane world of politicians

Many political discussions I've been involved in take the form of: "Why doesn't my representative do this?" or "Why don't Democrats do that?"

Several common complaints are:

- Why aren't they acting faster on a specific issue?
- Why aren't they changing things more?
- Why didn't they do _____?

Democrats are politicians. Politicians figure out, given the current environment, how to get elected, how to do what they can for the public given the current environment, and how to get re-elected.

One of the more popular ways Democrats have figured out how to do this is by triangulating towards a center. They often do this because any single candidate doesn't have the resources to change the landscape.

Some Democratic politicians work to influence the landscape, many do not. Regardless, the movement for change is more effective if it comes from people.

The Mackinac Center describes the situation in this fashion [Mac14]:

> Many believe that politicians move the [Overton] window, but that's actually rare. In our understanding, politicians typically don't determine what is politically acceptable; more often they react to it and validate it. Generally speaking, policy change follows political change, which itself follows social change. The most durable policy changes are those that are undergirded by strong social movements. ...
>
> The Overton Window doesn't describe everything, but it describes one big thing: Politicians will rarely support whatever policy they choose whenever they choose; rather, they will do what they feel they can do without risking electoral defeat, given the current political environment shaped by ideas, social movements and societal sensibilities.

But what about the Republican Party, you say? They change the political landscape.

No. They don't.

Corporations change the landscape. They change it for Republicans and Democrats; the Republican Party has simply been on the leading edge of embracing corporate special interest groups since at least Reagan. As a politician, it's an easy choice when you immediately reap the benefits of corporate lobbying groups like the Chamber and billion-dollar corporations like NewsCorp and ClearChannel working on your behalf.

If we want the landscape to change, we need to recognize the situation that many politicians are in: It's very difficult to do anything if large corporate special interest groups oppose it.

There are still advocates for the people in our government, but if you speak out against groups like the Chamber, you risk funding. If we want the landscape to change, we're going to have to do it ourselves.

Lawrence Lessig writes that to understand Washington, you need to understand the situation politicians are in and how corporate special interest groups make their life easier [Les11]. Politicians are judged these days, not by what they do in office, but by how much funding they bring to their party. Funding is needed to elect party members and get the party message out; the belief is that message and name recognition gets you to the magical 51% needed to win an election.

Here's how Lessig articulates influence in Washington:

> Members of Congress get access to desperately needed campaign cash—directly from the lobbyists, as facilitated by the lobbyists. They need that cash. That cash makes much simpler an otherwise insane existence, as it cuts back at least partially on the endless need of members to raise campaign funds elsewhere.

The problem, however, is that expectations come with these contributions. The expectations are not spoken aloud in a *quid pro quo* fashion, but are implicitly understood. The expectation is that the special interest will get something in return.

Here's the situation in a nutshell:

- Politicians need to win elections (get to 51% of the popular vote).

- Money wins elections.

- The people willing to provide the most money to politicians are the ones who stand to gain the most from legislation (if you can make $100 million from a particular piece of legislation such as a tax cut, it makes perfect sense to invest up to $100 million in order to realize a return).

- We get legislation that benefits special interest groups.

The Glass-Steagall Act is repealed under President Clinton. Drug companies gain full retail prices for wholesale purchases under George Bush's prescription drug plan. This same requirement remains under the passage of the Affordable Care Act (ACA). President Bush (and President Reagan before him) pass a series of tax cuts that primarily benefit the wealthy. Estate taxes are repealed. President Clinton passes NAFTA and welfare reform. The list goes on and on.

The problem isn't big government or small government. The problem isn't Democrats or Republicans. The problem is the political system—what it takes to win elections, the role special interest groups play, and the influence this buys them.

In order to fix this problem we need to break the chain of incentives ... somehow.

I believe the way to reduce the impact of money in the equation is to change the landscape. Change it so that we vote for candidates who believe in democracy. Change it so that politicians don't need such absurd amounts of money. And hold them accountable if they pass legislation for special interest groups.

The way to change the landscape is to define a core set of values, a core set of beliefs, and then work to elect people with these beliefs.

I think this would help our politicians immensely. They could do more if the political climate were different and they didn't have to worry so much about fundraising.

As far as elections go, it's as simple as this:

1. Vote in elections for the politicians who best represent our values and are capable of winning.

2. Find even better candidates to run in the primaries.

3. Support and promote these candidates.

4. Vote in primaries for the politicians who best represent our values and are capable of winning.

5. Repeat.

This system of change merely requires that we know and teach values like democracy, we identify candidates who match our values, and we support them as much as we can with at the very least our votes.

If the idea of a set of values makes you uncomfortable because you believe everyone should determine their own path, remember that this belief itself is a value. Why is it ok to watch a comedy show like *The Colbert Report* where everyone watching has similar beliefs and values yet it's somehow not "acceptable" to talk about these values and why they're important?

If this sounds like a lot of work to you, ask yourself how much time you spend playing the divide-and-conquer games of the special interest groups. What if we used this time teaching and learning about our values and the values of our candidates?

We endlessly construct and deconstruct policy solutions that will largely remain pipe dreams because we spend so little time on a system of change for making them possible.

What if we invested as much time in a system of change as we do debating all of the changes we want to happen? What if we prioritized winning people over to a better vision over playing right versus left or any of the other divide-and-conquer games?

PRACTICE

2.1 Pick an issue like money in politics. Using the concept of the Overton Window, how would you make this idea desirable or undesirable? What might the endpoints and range of possible solutions look like?

2.2 When it comes to politics, what beliefs do you hear being expressed in the media?

2.3 What are your values? What do you believe in? Remember, even a negative belief is a belief. Where do you hear others talking about your beliefs?

PART II

CHANGING THE GAME

CHAPTER 3

THE GAME OF "51"

Real rebels, as far as I can see, risk things.
                            —David Foster Wallace, 1993. [Wal93]

What to do?

As you may have guessed, I like to talk with people. It didn't come easy for me. I'm not a natural.

Because I'm not a natural, it fascinates me. So over the years I've practiced and turned it into a game. I like to think of it as a game because games are fun, games help you learn, and when we talk about politics we should be having fun and learning. Rather than trivialize the issues, I've found that thinking of political discussions as a game takes the pressure off and makes it easier to have conversations.

As I've practiced and played and found things that work, I've written them down.

I call this game **51** because this is the percentage of the electorate needed in a democracy for a majority vote. It's also the number of people I try to personally target. The rules are simple.

3.1 Goals

The goals of the game are:

1. Meet new people.

2. Win people over.

3. Learn and improve.

4. Encourage new players.

3.2 Why play?

Our strengths as people (the 99%):

1. Numbers.

2. Values: I feel we have better beliefs; selling a philosophy that only benefits a few people at the top is a difficult task.

3. Collaboration.

4. Bottom-up organization: We are strong at the grassroots level. We are local.

People win in a democracy when they are involved and participate.

Our weaknesses:

1. Money/corporate backing.

2. Media: We don't own much media.

3. Wedge issues.

4. Bottom-up organization: We tend not to value hierarchical, centrally driven organizations. This means we often struggle to coordinate across many groups.

For years, winning the money game has been the political strategy of both major parties: Democrat and Republican.

I believe it's time to declare this strategy compromised. It's compromised because we end up with politicians who serve the interests of wealthy special interest groups and we lack a party willing to challenge the radical ideas put forth by groups like the Chamber, the Cato Institute, ALEC, and The Heritage Society.

In general, corporate special interest groups rely heavily on one strategy: divide and conquer. We win when more people participate and when we unite around common goals and values.

Towards this end, what's needed is a distributive strategy that takes advantage of our strength in numbers. As corporations have devised strategies to shift the goal posts more and more in their favor, we need strategies to influence values and beliefs.

Does this mean we need the same strategies? I don't think so. I don't think adopting the same strategies will work because our values are quite different. We need strategies to counteract corporate influence.

We win when people participate. Corporate lobbyists win when people become apathetic.

51 is a distributive strategy to shift the political landscape.

3.3   You have nothing to lose

Did I mention that people are going to lose the money game?

If we know we're going to lose the money game, why do we keep trying to play the money game?

In other words, it's time to try some different tactics to break free of the money game. Because we're going to lose the money game, we have nothing to lose by trying something different.

To me, this rule is tremendously freeing.

We're going to make mistakes. That's OK. Treat it as practice. In this game, the idea is to learn about your values and build connections.

We're going to lose much more if we keep switching back and forth between Republican and Democratic parties trying to play a game that we've

Figure 3.1   Seriously.

been losing for 40 years as the center shifts ever further in the direction of corporate special interest groups.

3.4 Ground rules

A few ground rules:

- If it makes you angry, take a break.
- Focus on frames, ideas, and values.
- Remember that your goal is to win people over.
- Hold the moral high ground.

What's the moral high ground?

It is, in a sense, being in the "right." Not necessarily in the sense of a more correct or better argument, but in the sense of "doing the right thing." It means being true to yourself and to your values. In many ways, it determines political action.

Every time I talk about ground rules someone inevitably takes these to mean that the strategy is about being nice to people. I've heard everything from "You catch more flies with honey than you do vinegar" to people attacking me for what they perceive as being nice to an enemy.

While I'm told I am nice, this isn't about being nice. It's about holding the moral high ground. If you hold the moral high ground, you can ask for respect in return (even demand it if necessary) and if people refuse to give it to you, make them look like assholes. Not by calling them assholes, but by letting them *be* assholes. If someone wants to be an asshole, I'm happy to let them look like an asshole because the majority of people will side with me.

Too often, however, we fall for the liberal baiting and call people stupid instead of sticking to our beliefs. The moment you take the bait, *you* look like the asshole.

A few ground rules that take advantage of our belief in collaboration and community:

- If something works, share it.

  - Blog, post, discuss, or write.

  - Don't be afraid to talk to your friends and family about values; it's much easier than politics. Just be respectful of boundaries.

- Celebrate successes.

- If you see someone struggling, help them (don't stand idly by).

- Support alternative and independent media.

A few don'ts:

- No name calling.

- Don't play the Democrat/Republican game; this goes along with no name calling.

- Don't patronize corporate media. Don't pay for it or click on it if you don't have to. Think before reposting corporate media: Is this for shock value? Do you want to give them the publicity? Are you helping them make money?

- If you do watch corporate media, watch to understand how they sell corporate values. How do they try to marginalize traditional American beliefs? How do they take fringe, radical ideas and make them more mainstream?

- Don't take the bait and respond with outrage. If you must respond, challenge corporate values or strongly state your own beliefs.

Figure 3.2   Scoring at Dunster Archery competition. [IDS09]

3.5 Target and goal

Remember, not only is it easier, but talking to independents and people who see themselves as liberals about values and democracy is more productive. Given that people win when people participate and vote, think about where your energy is best spent.

Before you engage, you need to identify two things: **target** and **goal**.

Your target is the person(s) you want to win over. Your goal is what you want to achieve. The long-term goal of **51** is to win people over and create new players. Towards this end, however, there will likely be a series of short-term goals. These short-term goals should all directly relate to the overall long-term goal and will vary depending on your target.

A quick example.

> You have a good friend who's told you she doesn't like to discuss politics. You have an established relationship with this person. Your friend has great ideas and you would like to see her become more involved. So your long-term goal might be to help this person become more interested and engaged. A short-term goal might be to find an example where people getting involved made a difference. Another short-term goal might be to find out why she doesn't like to discuss politics.

Goal and target are important because they help you determine your approach.

They also allow you to set criteria for success. Remember, just because a goal is easier doesn't mean it's any less valuable. A great example is convincing people to vote and vote persistently. Often, all that's needed is a friendly reminder. Easy enough, right?

By setting realistic goals and targets, you don't waste time and energy and you keep morale up. Realistic goals help you avoid non-productive conversations.

3.6   But it's only 51 people ...

True. But if I can convince 20 out of 51 to play and those 20 can convince 20, you've already seen how quickly we have a network that rivals the corporate values communication network.

- 1st round = 20 people

- 2nd round = 400 people

- 3rd round = 8,000 people

- 4th round = 160,000 people

- 5th round = 3,200,000 people

- 6th round = 64,000,000 people

Quickly, we would have a significant voting bloc.

So we can make excuses or as I opened this book with, we can realize that we're six rounds away from reaching 64 million people.

Not only that, but in this distributed strategy we create leaders along the way. For example, at round 5, we have 3.2 million leaders. If we could get to 3.2 million leaders, I'd take my chances against any amount of money.

This is important because corporations own the media. Corporate-owned media will work to discredit and marginalize any single leader or organization that mounts a serious challenge to the corporate power structure.

Distributed leadership also allows for action along many local fronts. In this book, I'm focusing on winning people over in a distributed fashion and creating small localized networks. However, as you build your network, opportunities for action will arise at many different levels: national, state, local, and so on.

By building your network you will become aware of more opportunities and be more equipped to respond appropriately. Thinking about how to shift the landscape will help you identify which opportunities are most important.

3.7   8 goals that are easy to accomplish

These goals can be accomplished with minimal effort, and if done by enough people, help create a system for change.

3.7.1   Vote

Not only in elections but in primaries. On issue after issue, people are the new silent majority. Government policy would advance in the direction of people if we just voted consistently for politicians who represent the interests of people. This is why corporations spend so much of their time trying to convince people that their vote doesn't matter.

If voting doesn't matter, why are corporations spending so much time trying to prevent people from voting? Why do they encourage people who will vote for their issues to vote?

Remember, the problem is money's influence on politics. The less we vote, the more influence money has on an election. The more we vote and the more we vote for populist candidates, the less money will matter in elections.

Politicians are working for corporate special interest groups because corporate special interest groups have convinced them that the money they provide wins them elections.

Consistent voting for better candidates would have a ripple effect. The less money matters, the more we would get better, less corrupt candidates.

3.7.2   Convince others of the importance of voting

You've made it a point to vote consistently, now help others understand the importance of voting. Talk about what happens when people vote. Look at

Figure 3.3   Casting ballots in Washington, D.C., 1938. [Har38]

how easily President Obama was re-elected in 2012 when people turned out to vote despite the huge sums of money spent against him.

Or talk about corporate strategies to prevent people from voting like Voter ID laws and demotivational propaganda.

I know it can be frustrating to vote, especially if it seems like your vote doesn't matter or that the candidate you didn't do enough. The thing to keep in mind here is, did or will that candidate move the needle in the direction of the people. Any movement in the right direction is worth a vote.

The question shouldn't be: Did this candidate do X? The question should be: Is this candidate working to shift policy in the right direction?

We need candidates who aren't bought, sold, and delivered by corporate interests. The only way to do this is to get people out to vote consistently for better candidates. And yes, I understand there are Democrats who tow a corporate line. If we would vote more often in primaries for better candidates, we'd see candidates start to get braver.

Look at your list of 51 people, and figure out who you can talk to about the importance of voting.

3.7.3   Speak about your values

As discussed earlier, people make decisions based on conceptual frames. When it comes to politics, these conceptual frames are people's values.

You will not win someone over who holds a different worldview by presenting facts that refute their conceptual frame. Simply put, you will not win someone over by telling them that theyre wrong.

If you present people who believe in the idea of "free markets" the wonderful data and conclusions of Thomas Piketty, they are going to tell you that the solution is to make the markets "freer." Within their worldview, markets are natural things not to be "interfered with." Until you're able to reframe markets as man-made creations, the analysis will only be viewed as "interference."

When you speak about your values, you present a vision of the world you would like to see and are working towards. If your vision is compelling enough, people will want to work with you. (*Chapters 4-10* discuss some ideas about vision with examples to help.)

Talking about values brings people together, whereas refuting ideas only plays into the divide-and-conquer strategies of corporate lobbyists. These groups use divide-and-conquer strategies because their values are weak and radical. No one thinks wealthy people need more help, for example, except corporate lobbying groups.

If enough people speak about our values, we shift the window of options back in our favor. We elect better representatives. And we would see politicians of all stripes more willing to work towards solutions that benefit people.

Remember, politicians react to the political landscape and will do what is necessary to win elections. Corporate interest groups have changed the landscape to provide political cover for favors like tax avoidance. The way to change things is to change the landscape so these political favors look like the corruption they actually are.

If we truly believed in democracy, for example, and that unlimited campaign donations corrupt elections, we would elect representatives that believe in democracy and working for the people (or we'd put rules in place limiting how much corporations can contribute). If we always voted for the person who took the least amount of campaign contributions, eventually campaign contributions wouldn't matter. Eventually, politicians would avoid campaign contributions.

And yes, I know this is a stretch right now. But I also know that starting with values is the way to make it happen. You know how I know? Because there was a time when it would have been inconceivable to do many of the things that are on the table today. There was a time when privatizing our schools would have been unthinkable. There was a time when tax cuts for the rich would have been viewed as morally reprehensible. There was a time when gay marriage would have been unthinkable. There was a time when women's rights would have been unthinkable.

To me, the term moral high ground is intricately linked with values and respect. You earn respect by talking about what you believe in and treating other people with respect. If you treat people with respect, you are in a position to ask for respect in return.

You hold the moral high ground when you work to win people over. You hold the moral high ground by talking about your beliefs and values, not by calling people stupid or playing the Republican/Democrat game. You do this by speaking about your values. (*Chapters 4-10* provide help and examples.)

This isn't to say you should never be angry. There are times when you will be angry. Remember the goal of winning people over, though. Use your anger effectively. You don't win people over by calling people stupid. If something makes you angry, either confront it in a way that's productive or step away from the conversation.

The way to influence the direction of change is to start with values.

> Only collective moral force can unite the world.
> —*I Ching, Book of Changes*

3.7.4   Focus on those you can win over

Too often we spend our time and energy on people who we're never going to win over. They make us angry and we can't seem to understand the views they hold so we focus all our time and energy on them.

This is why I recommend focusing on people who you can win over. Focus on your friends. Focus on your family. Focus on independents or those who share a frustration with how corrupt Washington has become.

Look at your group of 51 people and identify those that you're most likely to win over and start with some easy goals.

Put the vast majority of your time and energy into lifting up and encouraging these people, rather than beating your head against the wall on someone you know you will never win over. The difficult part is that from an emotional standpoint, we often want to fight with the people who make use the angriest.

Imagine what our country would look like if we spent our time and energy on winning people over rather than spinning our wheels on ineffective Republican/Democrat fights.

3.7.5 Identify representatives with similar values

To move our country closer to a democracy that works for people (and not just corporate special interests and the wealthy), we need people and politicians who believe in democracy as a core value and will work for democracy.

Political affiliation no longer tells you whether someone is working for corporate special interests or not. Reporters should be asking candidates about their beliefs and campaign contributions. If they're not, ask them to—put it on their agenda. And if reporters won't ask, find out for yourself. Meet the candidate. Listen to what they say and ask questions at any possible opportunity.

We need candidates who are not corrupt. We need candidates who believe in democracy as a first principle and who are not working for corporate special interest groups.

We should ask candidates specifically about their beliefs in democracy and about their campaign contributions.

Some tell-tale signs that your representative works for people and not corporate special interest groups:

1. Your representative publicly states a belief in democracy.

2. Your representative believes in an economy that works for everyone, not in trickle-down economics (give to the top and the benefits "trickle down").

3. Your representative believes we have an obligation to ourselves and to others (mutual responsibility).

4. Your representative believes the United States is a good investment.

5. Your representative isn't waging a culture war.

6. Your representative believes we are all equal.

7. Your representative wants to limit the influence of money on democratic institutions.

8. The list of items your representative cares about isn't the same as the list at the U.S. Chamber of Commerce (or other corporate special interest group).

9. Your representative believes that government is by and for the people of our country—all of them.

3.7.6 Share

Share examples of beliefs and values. The best examples are ones that challenge corporate frames and replace them with better conceptual versions.

One of my favorite memes is shown in Figure 3.4.

There's plenty of work that needs doing in our country. We need better schools and less crime. Bridges are falling apart, parks need keeping up, highways need to be repaired. We need new technology like high-speed Internet broadband and we need to find alternative sources of energy before the oil runs out.

What kind of world has all this work but no jobs?

The beauty of this post is that it illustrates all of the things we could be working on if we weren't so focused on profits for a few people.

The reason we're not doing it isn't because it wouldn't benefit us. The reason we're not doing it is because a few people at the top who've benefited the most from our country don't want to pay it forward. A few people don't want to pay for our country because, well, "they got theirs."

Memes like this contrast with the corporate values espoused by people like Donald Sterling:

> **V. Stiviano:** Do you know that you have a whole team that's black, that plays for you?
> **Donald Sterling:** You just, do I know? I support them and give them food, and clothes, and cars, and houses. Who gives it to them? Does someone else give it to them? Do I know that I have ... Who makes the game? Do I make the game, or do they make the game? Is there 30 owners that created the league?

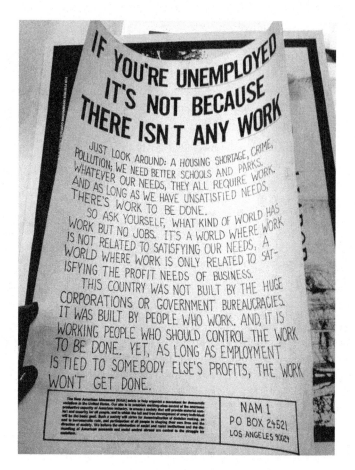

Figure 3.4 If you're unemployed, it's not because there isn't any work.

Right ... people watch basketball not because of all the talented people like LeBron James, Kevin Garnett, Chris Paul, or others. In Donald Sterling's world, the extremely talented people who work for him don't make him wealthy, he provides them with food, jobs, and houses. In Donald Sterling's world, people follow basketball because of Donald Sterling.

Making the ultra-rich richer doesn't have to be the goal of our society. There are much better goals that would benefit more people and make our country a much better place to live.

Another one of my favorites (Figure 3.5) points out the absurdity of having people who don't believe in democracy running for government.

Figure 3.5   If you don't believe in democracy, maybe you shouldn't run.

Examples like these are fun, witty, and speak at a values level.

They're examples that are very easy to share through social media and often won't wear out your friends with the right/left game. They're easy to repost.

It's also easy to bring up ideas like this with people in person. A great way to do this is by asking questions: Why are people who don't believe in government running for office? If elected, why would these people ever do anything for the people of our country? What's the incentive?

Successes are another great thing to share. Democracy (you remember our "by the people, for the people" government that countless other countries have used as a model for their own government) has been so demonized by corporate propaganda that we should point out the good things government does.

It's not the end all be all, but at the same time, our government is not the second coming of Stalin. And it would be a helluva lot better if we could return it to a government by and for the people.

Anyways, you get the picture. Think about creative ways to share your values because you may not see them in the corporate media.

3.7.7   Don't take the bait

How much time do you spend getting angry at someone who says something you don't agree with? How much time do you spend trying to convince people that they're "wrong"?

The answer may be, not much. But if you're like many of my friends, you engage in long drawn-out battles where you're constantly fact-checking some "conservative friend."

I'm going to make things easy for you. No amount of facts is going to convince die-hards. They've made up their mind and they are fighting a different war with you. They are fighting a war designed to draw you into the role of fact-checking liberal.

They do this a) to distract you from better goals, and b) so they can play the role of victim (of liberals who are always telling them that they're "wrong").

Turn off or ignore the corporate pundits; you know what they're going to say anyways: something to outrage you. Play a better game.

3.7.8   Lift up and encourage

You no doubt have likely seen or know people who are de-energized or demoralized from the fight against the well-funded, well-organized few.

The biggest frustration I've heard expressed is: How can people possibly think what they do? They waste enormous amounts of energy on trying to convince these religious people that somehow they are wrong and when they fail in convincing them, they often think that it's just not worth it.

This is why I suggest looking at the "low-hanging fruit," to steal a popular corporate phrase. Convincing someone to vote is relatively easy. Convincing someone to focus on those we can win over is even easier.

And when you start talking to people and realizing you help people attain these small goals, morale goes up instead of down. When people see small successes, they're more likely to both keep at it and push further.

This is true of any situation in life where you're learning how to do something.

Winning people over may be a bit of a new skill for people in your group of 51. That's why it's important to share your successes and talk about your failures. And if someone is struggling in some area, help out.

Suggest a different approach, suggest some options for an issue they're struggling with, or help them understand where best to focus their energy.

If you can help someone with a problem or issue they're experiencing, you become a leader, someone people look to for advice.

I put this in the low-hanging fruit category because most of the 51 people on your list are friends, family, or acquaintances. It's easy to encourage people you know. If they're down or struggling, forget politics and pick them up.

I've seen many people get down or frustrated because they are either a) in an argument they're never going to win or b) fighting with someone whose main goal is to frustrate them.

Disagreement is OK. You're not going to win every fight. Especially with someone fighting a religious battle. When you see people struggling in a situation like this, show them how to handle, avoid, or get out of the fights that aren't going anywhere. Help people understand how to talk about values and set reasonable expectations.

Energy begets energy when people hit goals and feel like they're making progress. Hitting these small goals will help build confidence that people can make a difference.

Remember, it's a marathon, not a sprint (both a truism and a cliché). Corporations didn't change things overnight. It took a major commitment to a value-based strategy over the course of 40 years.

3.8 My current "51" game board

The bulleted list is a quick snapshot of how I've broken up 51 people I want to target and some of the goals I've decided on with them. Obviously, not every individual will be the same as some goals will have been achieved, others in progress, and others outstanding.

Some goals are easy, some more difficult. Here's my list to help give you some ideas.

Target: *25 friends* who would currently describe themselves as liberals or Independents:

- Vote and help convince others to vote.

- Share their values more with friends and family.

- Become more involved in the community, even if just in a small way.

- Shift tactics from academic arguments to winning people over and articulating values/ideas (basically, the game of **51**).

- Hold the moral high ground.

- Support investment in public infrastructure, communities, and schools.

- Identify good politicians from bad (and support the good).

- Recognize corporate influence/corruption as the fundamental challenge facing our democracy.

- Stop fighting the right/left culture war.

- Describe how corporate media works (what corporate media will air, what they won't, how they operate).

- Recognize what makes an economy work and what we need to do to make it better.

Target: *10 acquaintances* who would currently describe themselves as liberals or Independents:

- Vote and help convince others to vote.

- Share their values more with friends and family.

- Become more involved in the community.

- Support investment in public infrastructure, communities, and schools.

- Recognize corporate influence/corruption as the fundamental challenge facing our democracy.

- Identify good politicians from bad (and support the good).

- Stop fighting the right/left culture war.

- Describe how corporate media works (what corporate media will air, what they won't, how it operates).

- Recognize what makes an economy work and what we need to do to make it better.

Target *10 friends or acquaintances* who view themselves as somewhat conservative:

- Share their values more with friends and family.

- Vote and help convince others to vote.

- Become more involved in the community.

- Support investment in public infrastructure, communities, and schools.

- Recognize corporate influence/corruption as the fundamental challenge facing our democracy.

- Recognize what makes an economy work and what we need to do to make it better.

- Expand their views of freedom and mutual responsibility (from selfishness and individual responsibility).

- Stop fighting the right/left culture war.

Target: *5 friends or acquaintances* who think of themselves as strong Libertarians or conservatives:

- Vote and help convince others to vote.

- Become more involved in the community.

- Support investment in public infrastructure, communities, and schools.

- Recognize corporate influence/corruption as the fundamental challenge facing our democracy.

- Recognize what makes an economy work and what we need to do to make it better.

- Expand their views of freedom and mutual responsibility (from selfishness and individual responsibility.

Target *1 insanely conservative person* I've been having an online conversation with for years:

- Develop mutual respect.

- Practice. I will never win this person over. However, he makes a great foil for practicing my ideas and framing. When I played tennis, I used to practice against a wall. I think of this person as my wall. Thanks to him I have written a couple articles that have been seen by more than 1 million people.

- He also keeps me up-to-date on all the latest corporate messaging.

- How great is this guy? Someday, I actually hope to meet him because we've become friends in a strange sort of fashion.

A few things to note. First, you might have noticed that none of my goals relate to a political party or political candidate. I'm not trying to convince anyone to vote for this party or that, or this candidate or that.

This is by design. I trust people will vote based on their values. I want to change the landscape so that we elect better politicians across all parties. In short, the goal is to shift all parties towards better values.

When you win the fight of ideas, you shift the entire conversation, you shift the Overton Window. Candidates from both parties will eventually support an idea if people start to value the idea and vote based on it.

Also, if we put all of our hopes into a single political candidate or party, if we lose this party/candidate, we have to start over from the beginning. This is why values and ideas are so important.

Second, notice that many of these goals are relatively simple. Convincing people to vote should be at the top of any list, for example. If we could just convince more people of the value of voting and repeat it for every election, we would have a much less corrupt government.

Third, you may have also noticed that I have more goals with my friends (people who I feel share the same ideas as me) than I do with those who don't. The reason for this is that I see that so many of them could be fighting better fights. I see them getting emotionally involved when conservatives bait them. I see them talking about policies when a better fight would be over values.

I see them overwhelmed and demoralized by sophisticated and extremely well-financed corporate divide-and-conquer tactics that they often don't recognize as sophisticated.

Figure 3.6 shows a post where several liberals expressed their frustration about conservatives not "getting it" when it comes to raising the minimum wage. Of course they don't "get it" because they believe markets will naturally, left to themselves, produce the greatest good.

The people protesting the minimum wage increase were, of course, reasoning from a "free market" cognitive frame where an unregulated market is deemed to produce the most "good."

Sam ▬▬▬▬▬

Facebook crashed on my phone while reading an ▬▬▬▬ post w/ people arguing why a minimum wage increase will hurt poor people. Makes sense.. Thanks for crashing! Yikes.

Like · Comment · Share · February 25 at 9:03am · 🔊

👍 ▬▬▬▬▬▬▬▬ and 6 others like this.

▬▬▬▬ Ugh
February 25 at 9:11am · Like · 👍 1

▬▬▬▬ Oh god...yeah, get outta there!
February 25 at 9:22am · Like · 👍 1

▬▬▬▬ That page is effed.
February 25 at 9:57am · Like · 👍 2

▬▬▬▬ Maybe we need to put the secret cabal back together.
February 25 at 12:31pm · Like

▬▬▬▬ surely this is nothing an emergency GA can't rectify
February 25 at 12:35pm · Like · 👍 2

▬▬▬▬ they are the same fools on the left, that claim that obama care hurts the poor, because they support universial healthcare, which will take a long time, if ever, and my family can not wait .we need health care now.
February 25 at 3:38pm · Like

▬▬▬▬ That thread was a joke......
February 25 at 8:17pm · Like

Figure 3.6   Liberal commiseration.

Instead of recognizing the frame that was being used and talking about minimum wage within the context of a better economic frame, they fought the typical fact battle. The resulting frustration ensued.

When you see frustration like this, it's an opportunity. Talk to them about better ways to frame the policy issue. Show them how to use facts within the context of better frames. And if they're really struggling, you may want to suggest some better, less frustrating and more positive uses for their time and energy.

In this case, because I didn't want to call out people who are my allies in a public forum, especially since I didn't know everyone, I talked with a couple of people in person and offline.

PRACTICE

3.1 Find a contentious political article online in either a national publication or local publication with a comments section. Read the comments. What games are being played/tactics being used?

3.2 Pick one close friend and identify a few goals you think you could accomplish with that person. What's one new thing that you might be able to convince him or her of? Examples include: importance of voting/participating, not playing the right/left game, the importance of talking about values.

3.3 Are people who describe themselves as conservatives your enemy? Are there any you know who you would consider trying to win over?

PART III

5 FRAMES FOR ANY SITUATION

CHAPTER 4

A BRIEF REMINDER ABOUT THE IMPORTANCE OF CONCEPTUAL FRAMES

There's always room for a story that can transport people to another place.
—J.K. Rowling, 2014 [Row13].

Have you ever wondered how Republicans manage to win people over despite having a philosophy that benefits those at the very top of the economic pyramid?

Recently, while canvassing, I struck up a great conversation with one of my neighbors. It turned out he knew not only national politics but also city and local issues and simply loved to talk politics.

While talking about the state of our state of Ohio, I brought up the recent budget cuts and the importance of investing in schools and communities.

He agreed completely but offhandedly mentioned how complicated it could be to talk about investing in communities. He asked the very prescient question:

Why can't the Democrats come up with simple issues like tax cuts?

I wanted to say that tax cuts really aren't a simple issue. It's actually a very complex frame that corporations have spent hundreds of millions if not billions of dollars developing and teaching over the past 40 years.

Tax cuts seem simple though because almost everyone, regardless of whether you're a conservative or a liberal, understands the frame. Just saying the two words "tax cuts" activates an entire series of associations. We understand this issue so well because it has been taught and repeated over and over and over and over.

This is why it appears simple. It isn't simple naturally. Everything is simple if you have a mental model for it.

What happens when I say "addition and subtraction"? You instantly evoke a mental model for how to add and subtract that you likely learned when you were young.

Imagine for a second trying to do addition and subtraction if you had never been taught how to add or subtract.

Or, to make the analogy a little closer to the actual situation, imagine trying to do addition and subtraction if someone had actually taught you division and multiplication and then called them addition and subtraction.

Tax cuts are simple to us not because they're simple. They're simple to us not because we really benefit from them.

They're simple because a conceptual framework has been put in place over the course of 40 years that allows us to understand tax cuts in the way that corporations want us to understand tax cuts.

When someone says *tax cuts* some of these thoughts likely come to mind:

- The 1970s recession and the Reagan tax cuts.

- People know best how to spend their money.

- Tax cuts grow the economy.

- George H.W. Bush's infamous "Read my lips, no new taxes" quote.

- Taxes are a "burden" on business.

- The Laffer Curve.

- The Bush tax cuts.

- Reducing the influence of "big government".

Keep in mind that I'm not saying any of this is true. The list is simply some of the components of the conceptual frame corporate special interest groups have created for *tax cuts*.

The logic built into this frame is that somehow tax cuts are always morally "good" and the right thing to do.

Enough, though, about corporate frames. You know them and you know they're not doing good things for our country (unless you count creating wealth and power for a few individuals as a good thing).

4.1   Criteria

I want to talk about a few frames for winning people over. Some will be more familiar than others. That's OK. The goal here isn't necessarily to create these frames but to dust them off and talk about how to use them.

There are many more but for the purposes of keeping it simple and focusing on five let's define a few criteria:

- It must be a positive vision. A vision is a goal to strive for; it is not a problem, attack, or critique. It is also not a policy prescription or solution. It is an end state. It is where we want to be.

- It should be as simple and powerful as possible.

- It should have a short descriptor to evoke the frame. Ideally, three words or less.

- It should focus on values.

- It should use and build on concepts we understand and currently use if at all possible.

- It should be highly extensible. That is, a good frame should be the backbone for many issues/solutions.

- A frame isn't an "—ism." It's not socialism, capitalism, communism, feminism, and so on.

- It should use powerful metaphors/language.

- A frame isn't a solution or policy recommendation. Solutions and policy recommendations come later. The frame should focus on a vision and values.

- It should be firmly grounded in research, science, and historical efficacy

- I must believe in it.

Now remember, you may have to do a bit of work upfront teaching these frames. Some will come easier than others. After introducing these frames, I'll also discuss some tips on how and when to use them.

Remember, a good conceptual frame is built from facts, but facts are not the same as a conceptual frame. Where relevant, I'll include citations to data and research I've pulled from that helped me build these conceptual frames.

The five frames I've found that best satisfy the above criteria are:

1. A working economy

2. Democracy

3. Mutual responsibility

4. Equality

5. Freedom

Some of these frames likely have a familiar ring.

4.2 Framing your own stories

Throughout the next five chapters on specific frames, I'm going to share some examples of values-based stories I've used that have worked for me.

My goal in sharing these stories is to help you think about how to create your own stories.

- What do you want to accomplish?

- What audience are you trying to reach?

- What does this audience believe?

- Is there a point of commonality you can start from with your audience?

- How will you talk about your beliefs?

- How can frames help you talk about specific policies or issues?

Towards this end, I'll do my best to talk about my **target** and **goal** with each example.

If a specific frame or story interests you more than others, feel free to skip around these chapters. Some you may be more familiar with than others. Some may help you with a particular policy or issue more than others.

If we can convince enough people to believe in a few visionary ideas, passing specific policies and legislation becomes much easier because the legislation "makes sense" within these conceptual idea frames. The way to convince the people you know is through the stories you tell.

Questions at the end of each chapter are designed to help you think about the story you want to tell.

CHAPTER 5

FRAME 1: A WORKING ECONOMY

I believe this is the defining challenge of our time: Making sure our economy
works for every working American. It's why I ran for President. It was at the
center of last year's campaign. It drives everything I do in this office.
                                        —President Barack Obama, 2013. [Oba13]

The deeply held belief corporate special interest groups push is that the
economy is a natural thing that will inherently do good, like electricity or
evolution. If you hold this belief, any attempt to improve the economy is
viewed as "interference" or "meddling."

Of course, these same special interest groups frequently meddle with the
economy to pass legislation for their own benefit.

One of the main goals of the corporate "free market" frame is to keep ordinary people from acting. In other words, to keep people from getting involved to create a better economy based on broad prosperity, rather than to benefit a few extremely wealthy people.

People have developed some good initial attacks on this conceptual frame. The 99% framing of Occupy Wall Street is alive and well as well as the income inequality framing of the problem.

Where we so often fail in discussions is that we don't offer a better vision about what the economy should look like. We present facts and then expect people to "compute" the right answer. The trouble is that often they're computing it through a different conceptual frame.

If the facts don't fit the frame, the frame sticks.

If you look at income inequality through a laissez-faire economic frame, for example, the solution would be: more deregulation. Even after the financial collapse of 2008, these economic frames persist because they haven't been challenged enough at the conceptual level.

Where I've had success in discussions about the economy is when I've contested corporate values about markets as entities found in nature and reframed them as things we created and have control over.

This is why, when I encounter someone who has bought into this view of the economy as natural, I start by establishing that the economy is something people created. It is not a god. It is not something that evolved in nature. It is a system of rules we have developed.

You're probably familiar with a few:

- The development of money after the barter system

- Property rules

- Rules of conducting transactions—agreement on price, payment, receipts

- Rules of incorporation

- Regulations for conducting business

- Rules prohibiting monopolies

We can create these rules any way we want towards any number of different ends.

Many of us take this for granted. However, in corporate framing, all of this is erased and the economy is framed as a natural thing.

If you establish upfront that we created the economy, this means we write the rules. We, the people, have this power. And strangely enough—I say strangely because this came as a surprise to me—after you do this you'll find that people feel much freer to talk about how we could improve things.

I suppose this is why the wealthy spend so much time telling us that we should sit back and let the magic of the free market work. What they really mean is, we'll write the rules, don't you worry your little heads.

The first step then towards a **working economy** or **working markets** is establishing that the economy is something *we* create.

After you've established that we created markets, you can introduce the idea of a working economy. Part of the beauty of the frame is that it is a vision, it is not a prescription for how to make the economy work.

What it does, however, is the opposite of the "letting the markets work" frame. It puts people back in control of writing the rules to fix the economy. It creates a vision to work towards and allows us the tools we need (such as economic experts and policy) to get there.

Here are some thoughts on the frame of a working economy:

- **Working** invokes the metaphor of operating correctly, instead of being broken. When a piece of machinery is not working, for example, it's worthless until it starts working again.

- A **working economy** is an attainable future state for the economy. It is a call to action: let's fix this thing!

- If an economy can be fixed, it means that we can fix it. We have the ability to make it **work**. This is extremely important because the conservative version of the economy is an economy that we can't control. The conservative worldview says "sit back, let the economy take control, and everything will be all right." The best course of action is no action. Ever wonder why many people are so compliant even as the wealthy work to re-write the rules so they can pay people less and invest less in our country? It's because the moral frame says that not only should we not do anything but that doing nothing produces the optimum outcome. Don't worry folks, the market will fix everything. Despite all the evidence to the contrary. This is the importance of changing the frame. The good news is that all of the evidence from

Figure 5.1   If our country were a car, it would look something like this. [Llo11]

the economic crisis says otherwise. This may be why people feel so uncomfortable; their conceptual frame is telling them to do nothing but everything they're witnessing is at odds with this view. We're told that market decisions will always be for the better, but our experience says otherwise. Our experience says that the economy is broken. Our experience says it's only benefiting a few people at the top. It's time to quit sitting idly by as the wealthy take more and more and invest less and less and fix it. This is an opportunity; we simply need to show people that markets are things we create and we can change the rules so they work better for more people. There has never been a better opportunity.

• The term 'working' also brings to mind the act of working, going to work, and workers. The economy should benefit everyone and not just owners.

5.1   Aspects of the working economy frame

Here, I'm going to keep this at a high level and avoid implementation details. Remember, this is a conceptual frame not an economic textbook. The idea is to lay out some of the aspects for a conceptual model of a working economy.

What would a working economy look like? What are some of it's principles?

Rules

A working economy has rules. It is not an anything goes free-for-all. It's more like our system of traffic lights and signs, which ensure traffic isn't a chaotic mess. Information needs to be equal between transaction participants. Because we create the economy, we create the rules. We can either do this so a few people benefit (the current situation) or so everyone benefits.

Fairness

A working economy works for more people. When everyone contributes, everyone should share in the benefits. Doctors would still earn more than retail clerks, but the disparity shouldn't be anywhere near what it is between, for example, a Walton family member and an employee at Walmart.

Money out of politics

Eliminate the money from politics. The vast sums of money have turned the tables so that our government is no longer working for people, but rather for certain wealthy individuals and corporations who are voting themselves breaks and benefits. We need to separate business influence from government so that government works for people again.

Equality

Everyone has an equal vote in a working economy. Period. Someone who owns a business isn't somehow "better" and deserving of more rights.

Infrastructure investments

For the economy to work, investments are needed in areas such as infrastructure, research, and education. A strong commonwealth is the basis for a working economy.

A living wage

A living wage is the minimum pay in a 40-hour work week necessary for someone to meet their needs. A living wage includes housing, clothing, and allows someone to maintain a decent standard of living within the community. When people earn enough to have a decent life, the overall economy benefits because more people can participate.

Equal regulations

Businesses will tell you that they want a level playing field. By this, they mean that it's difficult to compete with other businesses who have an unfair advantage. This unfair advantage could take the shape of less regulations, lower taxes, lower employee costs, and so on. What we are told, however, is that regulations are bad, taxes are bad, employee costs are bad. This is a special case of equal regulations called no regulations; you may have also heard of this as the race to the bottom. Why don't we ever focus on raising regulations and standards, equalizing taxes, and raising wages and benefits? Why don't we focus on bringing countries up to common standards? We should be focused on equal regulations.

Pay for productivity

- During the past 30 years productivity in the United States has steadily increased while compensation has stagnated and remained flat. The people doing the work are not realizing any of the benefits of increased productivity.

- Remember the promises of technology? The leisure time we all would enjoy after we no longer had to perform menial tasks? The utopia we would have on earth after automated factories? The artistic freedom we would have? The time with our families?

- A sign that an economy is headed on the path towards working is if people are earning more and working menial jobs less. Not the other way around.

Sustainability

A working economy has to be a sustainable economy for it to still work for future generations.

Now you may be starting to see the importance of focusing on the economy. It impacts just about every facet of our lives.

Imagine if we were fighting for a working economy instead of an economy that benefits the few. Imagine if we could say "working economy" and it had the same power as "tax cuts."

How much more successful would people be in achieving their goals?

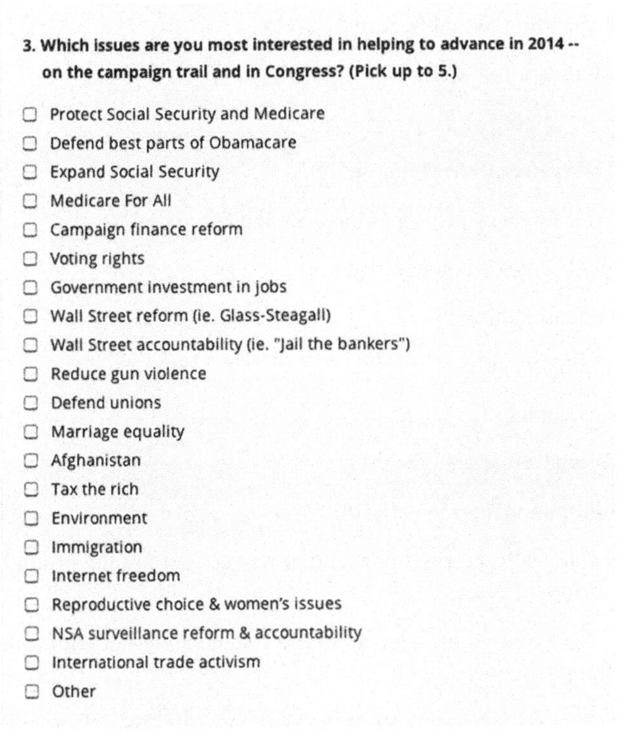

**3. Which issues are you most interested in helping to advance in 2014 --
on the campaign trail and in Congress? (Pick up to 5.)**

☐ Protect Social Security and Medicare
☐ Defend best parts of Obamacare
☐ Expand Social Security
☐ Medicare For All
☐ Campaign finance reform
☐ Voting rights
☐ Government investment in jobs
☐ Wall Street reform (ie. Glass-Steagall)
☐ Wall Street accountability (ie. "Jail the bankers")
☐ Reduce gun violence
☐ Defend unions
☐ Marriage equality
☐ Afghanistan
☐ Tax the rich
☐ Environment
☐ Immigration
☐ Internet freedom
☐ Reproductive choice & women's issues
☐ NSA surveillance reform & accountability
☐ International trade activism
☐ Other

Figure 5.2   2014 PCCC Questionnaire.

5.2   Issues/policies the working economy frame supports

The Progressive Change Campaign Committee (PCCC), a group I donate to that does much good work, sent out a survey of issues for 2014 (Figure 5.2).

The PCCC wanted to know which issues I supported in order to prioritize their resources.

I wanted to respond to them that I supported a **working economy**.

Why?

Here are the issues on the PCCC list that a working economy supports:

- Protecting Social Security and Medicare
- Defending best parts of Obamacare

- Expanding Social Security
- Medicare for All
- Campaign finance reform
- Government investment in jobs
- Wall Street reform (ie. Glass-Steagall)
- Wall Street accountability
- Defending unions
- Taxing wealth
- Environment
- Internet freedom
- International trade activism

If you start with the right conceptual frame, you lay the groundwork for a wide variety of issues.

Figure 5.3 shows some aspects of the social safety net within the frame of a working economy.

Within this frame, social security, Medicare, and the Affordable Care Act (ACA) all seem reasonable. The frame also helps people understand what options would be even better and what would be worse if they are interested in an economy that works for more people.

A belief in working markets also has the side benefit of helping to unite all of the various separate groups working on these individual issues. If you are an environmentalist, for example, and you could see how a working market would support your issue, wouldn't you be interested in fighting for working markets?

Here are a few other issues that **working markets** support:

- A living wage
- Health care for all
- Labor laws
- Wall Street regulations
- Net neutrality
- Monopoly busting

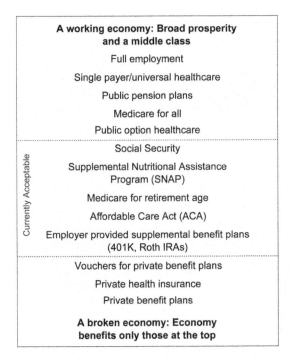

Figure 5.3   Overton Window for some social safety net options within a working economy frame.

- Small businesses
- Green energy

And there are quite likely many more. This is why I wanted to respond to the PCCC survey: I support a **working economy**.

5.3   How to use the working economy frame

This will vary depending on situation, but the first thing you always want to do is find out what people believe.

Do they, for example, believe that the economy is something people created?

If you don't know, literally, ask people about how they view markets. I know this sounds like an odd question, but conservatives have established the "let markets work" idea of the economy so well that often you have to break down this existing frame in order to get people to think a little differently about it.

Here are a few points you might want to bring up:

- Did the economy exist in nature? (Did dinosaurs trade?)

- Remember how people developed the barter system? How we developed money?

- How did President Franklin Roosevelt end the Great Depression? Hint: Federal spending through programs like the Works Progress Administration (WPA).

- Why is leaving markets alone the best thing to do? (What most people I've spoken with mean when they say this is "leave me alone.")

After you've established that the economy is something we created, you've often done the lion's share of the work. This may take some time because corporations have worked extremely hard to entrench this belief that markets know best. Baylor University conducted a poll in 2011 about beliefs and found that 22% of people believe that God guides markets [Dou11]. Even the non-religious, however, will typically tell you that the best thing to do for markets is to leave them alone.

Be patient. No one is stupid. They are simply reasoning from a different conceptual frame. Build a better frame for them. Remember, if you try to contradict them with facts alone, it's quite likely it will make their belief stronger.

If we have control over the economy, then we have the ability to either a) make it work for a few (what the few have been doing for the past 30 years), or b) make it work for broad prosperity. After you've established that markets are things we create that we have control over, you can then talk about how the economy is broken:

- All the benefits are going to a few at the top.

- The middle class is disappearing.

- Jobs are being outsourced to countries with lower wages.

- Resources are being used up without thought for future generations.

Talking about how the wealthy have been changing what markets mean may also help people realize that the economy is something we have control over. Corporate special interest groups are pushing to re-write rules to benefit them. Shouldn't we instead be pushing for rules that work towards a broader prosperity? Shouldn't we be pushing for a working economy?

The economy is broken and only benefiting a few. We need to stand up and say we want a working economy—an economy that works for more people.

Otherwise, we may get a slight change in policy here or there, a small increase in the minimum wage, or a new regulation or two for financial institutions, while the underlying philosophy of "free markets" remains the same.

Here, I've been pleasantly surprised in my discussions. People seem almost relieved when you empower them with the ability to make the economy work as if they've known all along that something is wrong but have been limited by this idea of helplessness before the market.

5.4   Example: The Affordable Care Act (ACA)

Target: "Free market" critics of the ACA.

Goal: Frame the ACA within the context of a working economy.

Here's how to talk about health care within the context of a working economy.

The health care market was broken, so we fixed it.

That's it.

Seriously.

You can elaborate more on it if you want. But the heavy lifting was done much earlier when we built a frame for the economy as something we created, we have control over, and that we want to work better for more people.

Instead of us being ruled by markets, we should be writing the rules that make the market work for everyone, not just a few. Markets are things we create (not gods) and we have every right to create them so they work.

When the health care market wasn't working for 30 million people, we fixed it. When U.S. spending was 17% of gross GDP, we fixed it. When the only option for many people was expensive emergency room care, we fixed it.

Do you see the power of framing?

The issue with many folks isn't that they don't have enough facts, it's that we're trying to argue something that violates their moral frame of leaving the market alone.

This is why it's so easy to talk about health care with people who already reason from the same frame and so difficult to talk about it when someone is reasoning from a different frame.

It is also why most of our typical arguments about health care fail. We offer facts that fail to fit the "free market" frame that corporate special interest groups have established, rather than first establishing a better conceptual frame for the economy.

Would as many politicians be running from the health care debate if we had a strong moral framework in place?

If we had built up this conceptual frame for the economy instead of assuming it, explaining the health care law would have been exponentially easier.

Of course, make sure that your frame is firmly grounded in science and reason. After you've raised questions about existing conceptual frames, you will need the facts and data to help make your case for a better frame.

Here, for example, I'd talk about the seminal economic work on health care, the 1963 paper "Uncertainty and the Welfare Economics of Medical Care" by Nobel prize-winning economist Kenneth Arrow [Arr63].

To summarize a few points:

1. Unlike most goods and services, people don't know when they'll need health care.

2. When people do need health care, it can sometimes be very expensive (for example, heart failure).

3. Patients typically don't know the cost of care (in economic terms, there is an asymmetry of information); they have no way of knowing how much a knee operation actually costs, for example. This increases the leverage of the health care industry over consumers and is sometimes why you'll see significantly different prices for the same services in different locations throughout the United States.

Items 1 and 2 make it very difficult for people to simply have the money available for health care in a manner similar to fires or natural disasters. This is why options are either government run or based on some type of risk pooling and insurance model. Given an insurance model, you simply can't have people opting in and opting out when they feel like paying.

I never lead with this information, however.

I've found that if I keep the discussion at a belief level, I often don't even need this other information. After people start thinking of markets as things we create and can fix, it's much more natural to come up with solutions.

If, however, you start with factual information on health care that contradicts the moral frame of "free markets," this typically only leads to a heated argument. If you start by establishing a "working markets" view of the economy, I think you'll find it's much easier to discuss policies like the ACA within that frame.

If people still choose to believe in "free markets," then you may be in a religious battle you can't win and may want to focus elsewhere. Sometimes people have other reasons for this belief, but often I've found people are looking for a sounder framework for the economy and find it a relief to hear that "free markets" aren't an economic truth.

5.5 Example: Why the Pope would be powerful even if he weren't Pope

> **Target:** Christians, Catholics, "free market" believers.
> **Goal:** Establish that people have the ability to shape markets any way we choose.

As Pope, obviously Pope Francis is a man who wields significant power. What I didn't realize until I started reading Pope Francis's writing is the sheer scope and power of his work [Aka14a].

There is a reason that Rush Limbaugh went after Pope Francis. Interestingly enough, it's the same reason Pope Francis was able to brush aside Rush Limbaugh's arguments as if he were a gnat (OK, a bloated gnat to be sure).

Pope Francis simply has much more powerful beliefs and is also able to frame them in a manner that puts Limbaugh to shame. Let's break this down.

At the heart of the corporate view of the economy is a belief. It's not an economic belief. It's a moral belief. It's a view of how things should and shouldn't work.

Figure 5.4 Pope Francis in St. Peter's Square. [Jim13]

The belief is in pure individualism and is often expressed when you hear anyone talk about "free markets."

George Lakoff explains that in a strict father family, the father is the decider. He is the head of the family and his authority must not be challenged. He provides for his family and disciplines them, with force if necessary, in order to shape them into proper moral beings [Lak04].

So how does this relate to markets?

Corporations are promoting a moral view of the world where the market itself is a version of "the decider."

Some people may accept and argue this belief without even thinking about it as a belief. It looks something like this:

- Let the markets decide!

- Capitalism = Freedom.

- Any involvement by government with markets is "interference."

Basically, all authority should be invested in markets and government should remain hands off.

You know the argument. You've likely encountered it in some way, shape, or form. If you have, you know how heated discussions can get as one way or another certain people may perceive you as trying to limit this "freedom."

According to Lakoff [Lak04]:

> The market is seen as both natural (since it is assumed that people naturally seek their self-interest) and moral (if everyone seeks their own profit, the profit of all will be maximized by the invisible hand). As the ultimate moral authority, there should be no power higher than the market that might go against market values.

Many conservatives have bought into this corporate idea of the market as the ultimate moral authority.

Think about this for a second. At the heart of corporate philosophy lies the belief that if everyone is selfish, somehow, and they can't tell you quite how, a world will emerge that will benefit everyone. You've also heard this phrased as "A rising tide lifts all boats."

Only it seems to be lifting a few boats while leaving the rest behind.

This belief in individualism alone and fundamentalist capitalism explains why many people feel that neither science nor government (nor anything else for that matter) should have any authority over the market.

5.5.1 Markets are not gods

This Pope would be powerful even if he weren't Pope because not only does he understand the importance of moral arguments but he's able to make the case like few others I've seen.

In his first writing of his papacy, Pope Francis points out the deification and false power attributed to markets [Pop13]:

> The thirst for power and possessions knows no limits. In this system, which tends to devour everything that stands in the way of increased profits, whatever is fragile, like the environment, is defenseless before the interests of a deified market, which become the only rule.

A deified market. I wish I would have said that. This is exactly the power some want to invest in markets when they say "Let the markets decide."

Do we really want to grant markets that much control over our lives?

Markets have allowed slavery in the past. Markets have allowed child labor. Markets have led to monopolies and vast inequality. Do we really want to get rid of laws prohibiting slavery? Do we really want to allow companies to hire children again? Do we really want to eliminate standards for our water and food?

Shouldn't we instead be saying "Let the people decide!" or "Let's do what's right!"

Francis reminds us of the importance of other values:

> Just as the commandment "Thou shalt not kill" sets a clear limit in order to safeguard the value of human life, today we also have to say "Thou shalt not" to an economy of exclusion and inequality. Such an economy kills. How can it be that it is not a news item when an elderly home-less person dies of exposure, but it is news when the stock market loses two points? This is a case of exclusion. Can we continue to stand by when food is thrown away while people are starving? This is a case of inequality.

He reminds us that the economy is broken and that fixing it is going to take more than a recovering stock market. He sets the criteria for a working economy as an economy of broader prosperity and an economy of greater equality.

Markets have no inherent ethics. Markets never weighed in on the morality of killing. Laws against killing exist only because people, working together as a government, decided that killing was a bad thing. Markets don't care one way or the other. Markets would simply set an appropriate price on a killing.

The same goes for inequality. When has the market ever weighed in on starving or inequality? Markets don't solve social problems. Markets for slaves looked like markets for fruit. Markets determine price and allocate resources.

Francis goes even further though:

> Behind this attitude lurks a rejection of Ethics and a rejection of God. Ethics has come to be viewed with a certain scornful derision. It is seen as counterproductive, too human, because it makes money and power relative. It is felt to be a threat, since it threatens the manipulation and debasement of the person. In effect, Ethics leads to a God who calls for a committed response which is outside the categories of the marketplace.

Pure capitalism is not only a rejection of ethics, but God. No wonder Francis has ruffled so many feathers here in the United States where corporations have been selling us supply-side Jesus for the past 40 years.

He is right though: Ethics exist outside of markets and should guide markets. Ethics are a part of working markets.

Compassion, caring, empathy, and feeling. Also outside of markets:

> To sustain a lifestyle which excludes others, or to sustain enthusiasm for that selfish ideal, a globalization of indifference has developed. Almost without being aware of it, we end up being incapable of feeling compassion at the outcry of the poor, weeping for other people's pain, and feeling a need to help them, as though all this were someone else's responsibility and not our own. The culture of prosperity deadens us; we are thrilled if the market offers us something new to purchase. In the meantime all those lives stunted for lack of opportunity seem a mere spectacle; they fail to move us.

It's not that markets don't care; it's simply that markets are *only* about trade while there is so much more to life than trade.

Yet we're told we should set everything outside of trade aside and somehow markets will magically deliver a better life for us all. Despite any evidence to the contrary, we're supposed to believe that somehow out there this great utopia awaits if we will just do nothing and let it happen.

Is the Pope socialist, or in Rush Limbaugh's words "pure Marxism"?

Here is how the Pope answered Limbaugh [Wil13]:

> The Marxist ideology is wrong. But I have met many Marxists in my life who are good people, so I don't feel offended.

What I really admire about Pope Francis is that he doesn't get upset with Limbaugh. He doesn't get defensive. He simply says what he believes and shows empathy for people who believe differently. He believes Marxism is wrong, but the people are good. In other words, he disputes the ideology rather than the people.

Then, he goes on to emphasize how he isn't against capitalism, only certain aspects of supply-side economics:

> The only specific quote I used was the one regarding the "trickle-down theories" which assume that economic growth, encouraged by a free market, will inevitably succeed in bringing about greater justice and social inclusiveness in the world. The promise was that when the glass was

full, it would overflow, benefitting the poor. But what happens instead, is that when the glass is full, it magically gets bigger nothing ever comes out for the poor. This was the only reference to a specific theory. I was not, I repeat, speaking from a technical point of view but according to the Church's social doctrine. This does not mean being a Marxist.

He points out clearly and succinctly what Limbaugh and other corporate hacks have been doing for years: labeling anyone who disagrees with them as socialist, communist, liberal, and so on.

The Pope simply reminded us of the failed promise of trickle-down economics, an idea with little backing from economists outside the Wall Street world, and how pointing this out does not make him a socialist.

Notice he didn't call Limbaugh an idiot. He didn't lose his temper. He simply held his moral ground.

This is the last reaction people like Rush Limbaugh want. The good news is you don't have to be Pope to do this. You can do this with your friends. When baiting is effectively countered by more powerful framing, people like Rush search for weaker folks to bait.

PRACTICE

5.1 What examples could you use to demonstrate that markets are things we create?

5.2 What issues/policies that you believe in would the frame of a **working economy** support?

5.3 Think about someone you know who believes in the "free market." Imagine trying to convince this person that markets are things we create (they didn't occur in nature before we created them). What examples might you use? What approach might you take?

5.4 One of my favorite analogies to use when talking about economics with people is the pirate ship. Imagine you are on a pirate ship. Talk about some of the roles: captain, first mate, cook, surgeon, sailors, gunners, cabin boy, cooper, and so on. Set the stage that you and your friend(s) are on a pirate ship and you manage to procure 1,000 gold coins. There are 40 crew members. How should it be divvied up? What should the investor who funded your voyage receive? What would be fair?

Relate this to the current distribution of wealth in our country. In 2010, the top 1% had 35.4% of the wealth in the United States. The next 19% had 53.5%. The bottom 80% had 11.1% [Wol12]. In pirate terms, this means, the bottom 80% or 32 lowest ranking crew members would have to split 111 gold coins. This is roughly 4 coins apiece. Or more likely more coins for those at the top and a coin apiece for the lowest ranks. The investor who funded the ship would receive 354 coins. And the top 8 ranking officers would split 535 gold coins, or roughly 70 gold coins each.

5.5　Find a current article about an issue you believe in. In the comments, state that you believe in a **working economy** to justify your issue. See how people respond. Remember, you might have to do a bit of work to set up the frame of a working economy.

5.6　Share your conversation about **working markets** with a friend or blog about it online (at a site like *Daily Kos* or other political forum).

CHAPTER 6

FRAME 2: DEMOCRACY

> We can have democracy in this country, or we can have great wealth concentrated
> in the hands of a few, but we can't have both.
> > —attributed to Louis Brandeis, Supreme Court Justice. [Dil41]

The good news about the conceptual frame of democracy is that you're quite likely already familiar with it. You're also familiar with the oppositional frame: laissez-faire capitalism.

In a nutshell, according to the frame of laissez-faire capitalism, we should always be working to shrink government in order to free businesses from the shackles of regulation. People acting according to their own self-interests will create the greater good.

The belief, at its heart, is that free market capitalism is the best form of government.

> Capitalism is the only system that can make freedom, individuality, and the pursuit of values possible in practice. When I say capitalism, I mean a pure, uncontrolled, unregulated laissez-faire capitalism with a separation of economics, in the same way and for the same reasons as a separation of state and church.
> —Ayn Rand, 1966. [Ran66]

You've heard this belief in the form of "markets regulate themselves." No laws needed, no regulations. In short, the idea is that government isn't needed (or we need as little as possible).

When I'm talking with someone and I encounter this conceptual framework, it's important to think about capitalism as a proposed form of government.

A few issues with capitalism as government:

- Voting with your dollars means that those with the most dollars have more votes.

- Power concentrates in the hands of a few.

- Corporations/private owners have no responsibility to the people. Or the future.

- As a form of government, capitalism ensures that those with the most money receive the most service. If we had a capitalist government, this would be true for education, for recreation, for opportunity, for police, for fire, for trash collection, and for any other type of public service. In a society with a capitalist government, the rich would have the best possible police protection, while the poor would have to protect themselves.

These are a few issues I typically bring up when thinking about capitalism as a form of government. Most people don't typically think of capitalism as a form of government, but this is what corporate interest groups have been advocating. For them, the light at the end of the tunnel is a situation in which they have more power than in a democracy—either corporate-controlled government or no government whatsoever.

After you start thinking about capitalism as a form of government, it's easier to compare and contrast it with democracy. Especially because most people are familiar with democracy.

The simple vision at the heart of democracy is that government is based on the consent of the governed. Democracy is government by and for the people. People are sovereign and hold the power and elect representatives to serve the best interests of everyone. These representatives are temporary, serving at the will of the people. Not only must they be elected, but elections occur periodically. Everyone has the right to vote and to participate equally.

In a democracy, citizens have an obligation to be informed about public issues, to watch over how representatives use their power, and to voice their own opinions and interests.

6.1 Aspects of democracy

A few other aspects of democracy:

Equality

> All citizens are equally important and have the ability to participate equally within a democracy.

A system of law

> Laws protect the rights of citizens, maintain order, and limit the power of government. In a democracy, no one is above the law.

Separation of power (checks and balances)

> Government is divided into branches: legislative, executive, and judicial, each with distinct areas of responsibility and each providing checks against any one branch or person gaining too much power. A good question to ask is: "What are the checks against a corporation or special interest group that has gained too much power (become a monopoly)?"

Separation of church and state

> Prevents state churches and establishes the freedom of religion. Jefferson writes [Jef98]: "Believing with you that religion is a matter which lies solely between Man & his God, that he owes account to none other for his faith or his worship, that the legitimate powers of government reach actions only, & not opinions, I contemplate with sovereign reverence that act of the whole American people which declared that their

legislature should 'make no law respecting an establishment of religion, or prohibiting the free exercise thereof,' thus building a wall of separation between Church and State."

Debate/freedom of speech

People are free to criticize elected representatives and to observe how they conduct the business of government. Towards this end, the Constitutional guarantees of free speech and assembly are important.

Organizational freedom

People also have the right to organize according to interests and beliefs: doctors, teachers, workers, students, trade groups, environmental groups, women, causes, cultural groups.

The commonwealth (or common good)

The common well-being, the public welfare or general good. The idea is that government should act in the best interests of everyone.

Collaboration

Because power is dispersed, collaboration is essential for progress. Collaboration, however, also extends to individual citizens as we organize around areas of interest to inform government.

Knowledge to inform positions

- Knowledge is critical to making decisions and participating in a democracy. Because control of knowledge can become an issue, people need access to knowledge that is independent and allows people to make decisions free from authority.

- Government knowledge should be transparent in a democracy. It should be clear how decisions are being made and how these decisions benefit people.

Clearly, there are more aspects to democracy. In fact, it would be very easy to write entire books on the subject as many have done.

6.2   Issues/policies democracy supports

Similar to the working economy frame, the conceptual frame of democracy supports a wide variety of issues:

- Limiting the influence of money in politics.

- Voting rights.

- Fair and nonpartisan elections: People must be able to vote free from intimidation and violence. To be fair, elections should be administered by a neutral party that holds no partisan favor. A process for handling disputes also needs to be in place.

- Free and independent media.

- Public education.

- Campaign finance reform.

- Ending government surveillance.

Figure 6.1 shows some aspects of campaign finance reform within the frame of democracy.

Democracy: by the people, for the people

Publically funded elections

Equal media access

Limits on issue campaigns

Matching funds

Limits on donations to parties

Limits on donations to candidates

No coordination between issue campaigns
and election campaigns

Candidates purchase media access

No limits on issue campaigns

Coordination between issue and election campaigns

No limits on party funding

No limits on candidate funding

**Corrupt government, by and for
the wealthy**

Currently Acceptable

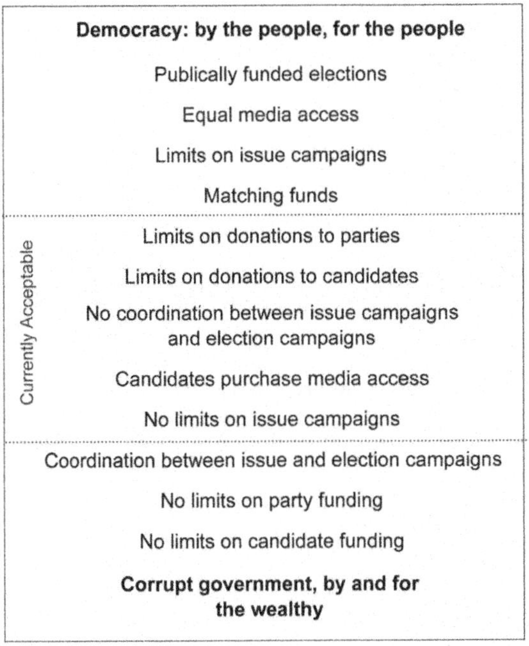

Figure 6.1   Campaign finance reform options within a democracy frame.

If we truly believe in democracy, our elections should be free from the influence of money. Within the frame of democracy, campaign finance reform makes sense.

6.3 How to use the democracy frame

Start by talking about the differences between democracy and markets as a form of government.

Many people who've heard corporate anti-government marketing haven't thought much about the end goal of markets as government.

Some questions to ask:

- In a market, how many votes do people get? How do you participate as a consumer?

- How many votes do you get in a democracy?

- Are markets responsible to the people?

- Do markets make good government?

- Don't markets reflect conditions of inequality rather than fix them?

  - Lower women's wages

  - Skill/wage gaps by race

- Did markets fix _____?

  - Slavery?

  - Winning the right to vote for women?

  - Child labor?

  - The Great Depression (Or more recently, the financial collapse)?

Talk about examples where eliminating government from markets has failed:

- Health care

- Financial markets

- Any tragedy of the commons example: environment, overfishing, water, peak oil, and so on

- Concentration of wealth

Establish that democracy is a better form of government than markets. This isn't to say that markets don't serve a purpose or do good. Democracy is simply a form of government whereas markets are markets. Markets don't establish laws, or resolve common resource challenges, or end monopolies, or resolve social problems, or create rules to make sure markets work for the benefit of our people and our country.

One of the claims I most often hear when it comes to any kind of government is: "I shouldn't be 'forced' to do anything." Where I hear this most often is when it comes to paying taxes.

This is, of course, ridiculous.

We are a nation of law. You don't get to pick and choose. You stop at stop lights because it's not just about you. You may say you want to kill someone, but you don't act on it because it's against the law. We have laws because we don't live alone in society; it's not just about you.

If you don't want to pay for our country, you should leave. Taxes are the dues of democracy.

I find it amazing that people who talk so much about how great America is and what a great country we have, don't want to pay for our country.

6.4 Example: Corruption in a democracy

> **Target:** Just about anyone. You can exclude people that already believe in democracy, but often I've found even they like this story because they can retell it.
>
> **Goal:** Establish a different frame for thinking about government instead of less/more and frame corporate influence as corruption.

Depending on the individual, you can shorten or lengthen this discussion as you see fit. Often, however, even with people who I think likely agree with me, I've found it's helpful to establish some common ground.

Here, I'll start with what's happened to our country over the course of the last 40 years. I start here because at a certain level, everyone seems to understand this situation.

To start, I draw the picture in Figure 6.2.

I usually sketch this on a napkin. The arrow from the top down symbolizes the power relationship. This drawing illustrates the influence of corporate special interest groups over our government. People are at the bottom of this power relationship.

Then I talk about an example or two to back up my case for corporate influence of government.

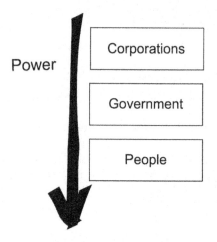

Figure 6.2   The problem: Corporate influence over government.

Here are a few to choose from:

- ALEC legislation

- The financial bailout of 2008

- Corporate lobbyists appointed to head major federal agencies (Tom Wheeler at the FCC)

- Insurance companies crafting health care legislation

- The West Virginia chemical spill and Freedom Industries

- K Street lobbying

- The Citizens United decision and the more recent McCutcheon vs. FEC decision eliminating limits on corporate campaign donations

I'm sure you can think of more. Most people pick up on this pretty quickly and start to say something like "Yeah, I get it, so what do we do?"

Don't rush to any recommendations yet. Ask for feedback: Does this, at a high level, sound about right?

If the conversation starts to veer into some type of right/left conversation, keep it focused on the situation. You may have to say something like "Let's just focus on the situation right now. Forget political parties."

The point here is that just about everyone seems to agree on the situation. If you've done nothing else, you both now agree on the issue.

6.4.1 Visions of the future

Now, let's talk about how we might fix this. Again, to avoid any kind of right/left fight, I'll say: "Let's start with the solution that no one is proposing."

I draw a different picture (Figure 6.3).

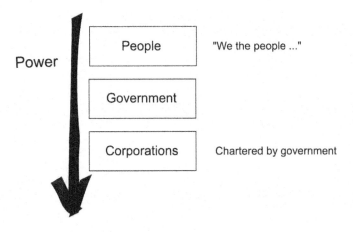

Figure 6.3   Corporations chartered by the people in a democracy.

In this one, people are at the top. I usually write "government of the people, by the people, for the people" next to people/government. You can also use "We the people ..." from the U.S. Constitution.

The important point is that government should be in the hands of the people. This is how our country was designed.

Equal representation. A system of checks and balances. A Bill of Rights to make sure the majority can't vote away individual rights.

I then write "chartered by government" next to corporations to highlight that corporations didn't even exist until we legislated rules for their existence in the 18th and 19th centuries.

The American colonists had not only freed themselves from England, but from the East India Company (EIC), a company larger and with more political influence in its day than Walmart today.

The Tea Act of 1773, for example, was designed to largely establish the EIC as a monopoly in America by undercutting prices of local importers and small American tea merchants. The Tea Act exempted the EIC from high British taxes charged on everyone else. Small American businesses had to pay the tax without having any say or vote in the matter ("No taxation without representation!"). [Har10]

For 100 years after our founding, America exercised strict control over corporate power. Charter companies were limited to special purposes (such as railroads) and were granted for only a limited time. Charters could be revoked for breaking laws and were prohibited from making political contributions and influencing lawmakers [Rec14].

It wasn't until the late 18th century that corporations transitioned from charter companies to private entities. The first limited liability legislation was passed in 1811 in New York state. Other states quickly followed suit to lure capital. In England, the Joint Stock Companies Act (1844) and the Limited Liability Act (1855) laid much of the groundwork for the modern day corporation.

The main point to get across is that we, the people, established a framework for both government and corporations. Neither just arose fully formed from the earth. They are what we made them.

We, the people, established a government so that we could be as free as possible as long as we weren't infringing on the freedom of others. We would govern ourselves through representatives, free from the tyranny of any sovereign or religion.

At the same time, there was a sense of the common good. Many of our early states actually chartered as commonwealths.

From the Commonwealth of Massachusetts Constitution [MA14]:

> The body politic is formed by a voluntary association of individuals: it is a social compact, by which the whole people covenants with each citizen, and each citizen with the whole people, that all shall be governed by certain laws for the common good.

You can hear this echoed in the Constitution in the Preamble and the general welfare clause:

> The Congress shall have Power to lay and collect Taxes, Duties, Imposts and Excises, to pay the Debts and provide for the common Defense and general Welfare of the United States; but all Duties, Imposts and Excises shall be uniform throughout the United States.

The purpose of government was to provide the infrastructure (rights, courts, resources, and so on) within which people could best pursue their goals.

How did we establish this freedom?

- Representative government: one person, one vote.

- Laws to be established for the common good by a bicameral legislature.

- Everyone is equal under the law.

- Branches of government to provide checks and balances.

- A bill of rights to prevent tyranny of the majority.

Add more or less as you see fit. This is just the structure I use. In reality, it's more of a conversation. Gauge your audience. Does this make sense? Are they seeing things similarly or differently?

I believe most people will largely agree up to this point though you may get some push back over the idea of a common good. Everyone I've had this conversation with has been pretty receptive though a couple tried to push me into the next sections, which compare and contrast the Democratic and Republican visions of the future.

Depending on your audience, you can switch up the next two sections. Sometimes I'll start with the corporate/Republican Party vision and sometimes the Democratic Party's vision.

6.4.2   The corporate/Republican Party vision of the future

The corporate vision is smaller (or no) government. Figure 6.4 shows a picture similar to Figure 6.1 with government reduced in size.

People are still at the bottom and lack the representation of corporations.

Here, I've found it's important to talk about scale. When people think about markets, they typically think about them as two individuals engaged in transactions on an equal footing.

Only this is far from the case.

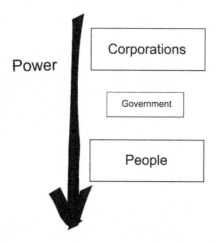

Figure 6.4   Smaller government doesn't fix the problem.

Corporations often have monopoly or near-government-like power (without any of the responsibility to the people). They have exclusive patents. Or they work out agreements for mutual profit not to compete. Or they have managed to obtain exclusive access to a valuable resource like water or a critical component of the Internet backbone.

An easy example is cable television. Companies like Time Warner Cable and Comcast don't compete and exist solely for profit. When profit is the sole purpose, incentives are strong to find ways to deliver less and charge more. In other words, to create monopoly conditions. This is why our country has some of the highest costs and lowest speeds for broadband in the world [Aka14c].

What I don't think most people realize is the implication of saying: "We should vote with our money."

It means your representation is greatly reduced. Venture capitalist Tom Perkins, without knowing it, expresses the sentiment perfectly:

> But what I really think is, it should be like a corporation. You pay a million dollars in taxes, you get a million votes. How's that?

The more money you have, the more influence you have. Isn't this taking us a huge step backwards from equal representation? Isn't this the very definition of corruption?

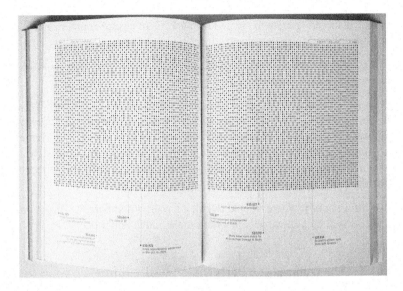

Figure 6.5   To represent 1 million, a book with 5,000 dots on each page would be 200 pages long. Your vote would be 1 dot on 1 page. [Her09]

The corporate special interest view of democracy tossed around by conservatives and attributed to Alexander Tytler and many others is[Col09]:

> A democracy will continue to exist up until the time that voters discover that they can vote themselves generous gifts from the public treasury.

However, it looks like what's happened is that certain corporate special interest figured out how to increase their leverage to purchase gifts. One of the ways to do this is through the idea of "smaller government."

This is why we've seen deregulation, consolidation, reduced choice, regulations written by industry, offshoring, union busting, and the defunding of government regulatory agencies. This is why we've seen the shifting of the tax burden onto individuals, net neutrality up for sale, federal bailouts, new anti-voter laws, and consolidation of monopolies.

Meanwhile people have experienced wage stagnation, reduced benefits, less competition, higher taxes, poorer service, and less representation.

The question I often ask is: Isn't smaller government just an argument used to increase corporate power?

I don't care so much about the size of government so much as the role of government. It should be by and for the people. It should serve the common good. It should operate to create fair markets, to ensure competition, and to make sure corporations behave ethically and for mutual benefit.

I care that we have sufficient government to make sure markets work for everyone, not just a few people.

This is why I believe we need to rethink where we are and where we want to be. I don't want a vision of our country where we shrink our government until it's completely ineffective and corporations can "drown it in a bathtub" to quote Grover Norquist, corporate lobbyist [Win13]. And I don't want a vision of our country that looks like poll-driven, marginal improvements on the back of a corporate vision.

I want a country where people decide. I want a democracy. Based on the past 30 years, I believe people would make much better decisions.

6.4.3   The Democratic Party vision of the future

Democrats typically don't tell a very good story when it comes to their vision of government.

Whether this is because they're afraid of offending corporate donors or whether it's because they simply assume people already believe in democracy, I don't know.

The problem is that without a strong vision of democracy, the corporate vision of no government (or limited government) gains traction and becomes the only vision.

By default, therefore, the Democratic vision of government is the corporate vision of government with some new policies thrown in to make it run slightly better.

Examples of policy modifications include:

- An increase in the minimum wage

- The Affordable Care Act (ACA)

- Immigration reform

The biggest issue here is that these policies are not a vision; they're policies. Lack of a strong vision is why Democrats often struggle explaining policies they want to enact.

The other issue is that the basic power structure is still the same. Corporations are still at the top of the picture with people at the bottom.

This is my biggest frustration with the Democratic Party: they talk about incremental change without presenting a vision.

Currently, without a vision, Democrats act like a party of mid-level managers chartered with enacting the corporate vision. In other words, where there's a vacuum of vision, this vision is filled by the corporate vision of smaller government.

To be fair, the Republican Party doesn't set vision either. The Republican Party simply adopts a pure corporate vision and doesn't even bring people into the equation.

Fortunately, presenting a vision of democracy is easy.

When you present a strong case for democracy, it's easier for people to see what's gone wrong. Subsequently, it's easy to make the case for a return to democracy where government is by and for the people and corporations are chartered for the good of people.

PRACTICE

6.1   Since our country was founded as a democracy, most people are familiar with the concept to some extent. Unfortunately, we often talk more these days about big or small government rather than democratic government. What are five aspects of democracy important to you?

6.2   Consider markets. What would a government look like that was only a market? What would it do well at? Where would it fail?

6.3   Think of someone you know who you'd characterize as an independent. Try drawing the situation in our country where government responds to corporate special interests over the needs of the people.

6.4   Share your conversation about **democracy** with a friend or blog about it online (at a site like *Daily Kos* or other political forum).

6.5   Find the Web site for your Congressional (state or national) representative. Usually, your representative will list the issues they believe in. Is democracy one of the issues? Contact them and ask them to fight for democracy.

6.6   Why don't more politicians list democracy as a belief?

CHAPTER 7

FRAME 3: MUTUAL RESPONSIBILITY

If I am not for myself, who will be for me?
If I am only for myself, what am I?
And, if not now, when?

—Hillel the Elder, 110 BCE 7 CE. [Hil00]

When opening up my notes on mutual responsibility one day, I found this quote from Hillel with no explanation nor link to where I had found the quote.

I knew why I had written down the quote though.

I found it a particularly well phrased way of explaining the balance between caring for one's self and caring for others. In other words, Hillel articulates quite beautifully the concept of mutual responsibility.

It's important to realize that it indeed is a balance because corporate moral framing, via Ayn Rand, posits two possibilities: selfishness and altruism. Rand argues for selfishness claiming that all of the previous world religions stem solely from altruism. In corporate frames, your only actions are consumer actions.

I wonder if Rand knew about Hillel, one of the most important figures in Jewish history. He founded the House of Hillel and helped develop both the Mishnah and the Talmud.

His teachings are at the heart of Judeo-Christian thought, which Rand ham-handedly characterizes as altruistic. Yet Hillel preaches balance.

We must not only be responsible to ourselves, we are responsible to others. It's this "responsibility to others" portion of our values that Ayn Randian corporatists want to erase in favor of the idea that somehow pure selfishness leads to a greater good.

At the core of our concept of society is this idea that we are mutually responsible for one another, that we are our brother's keeper. It is therefore society itself that corporate propagandists seek to destroy.

The reason? Selfishness is a convenient philosophy for justifying absurd wealth.

To restore balance, we must value our responsibility to others along with our responsibility to ourselves.

> I have now reached the point where I may indicate briefly what to me constitutes the essence of the crisis in our time. It concerns the relationship of the individual to society.
>
> The individual has become more conscious than ever of his dependence upon society. But he does not experience this dependence as a positive asset, as an organic tie, as a protective force, but rather as a threat to his natural rights, or even to his economic existence.
>
> Moreover, his position in society is such that the egotistical drives of his make-up are constantly being accentuated, while his social drives, which are by nature weaker, progressively deteriorate.
>
> All human beings, whatever their position in society, are suffering from this process of deterioration. Unknowingly prisoners of their own egotism, they feel insecure, lonely, and deprived of the naive, simple and unsophisticated enjoyment of life. Man can find meaning in life, short and perilous as it is, only through devoting himself to society.
>
> —Albert Einstein, 1943. [Ein49]

7.1   Aspects of mutual responsibility

A few aspects of mutual responsibility:

Empathy

> To understand yourself, you must also walk a mile in another's shoes. As you come to know more people and develop relationships with them, you come to understand them, value them, and feel a sense of responsibility to them as you do also to yourself.

Cooperation

> Mutual responsibility leads to groups organizing together for their common benefit as opposed to selfishly competing against each other. 21st century challenges like climate change, peak oil, and worldwide depletion of resources, in all likelihood, will require cooperation on a new scale and reach.

Respect for others

> Though we may have our differences, we have far more in common than we often think. Most people want certain things out of life: happiness, family, relationships, freedom, and the ability to grow as human beings. Respect comes when we recognize that we're all more similar than we think and deserving of respect in areas where we differ. To paraphrase the Bible, "treat others as you would like to be treated."

Trust

> When people trust each other, they can have honest conversations and work together towards common goals. Whenever possible, look to build trust through shared interests and respect. Mutual responsibility leads to cooperation.

Self-awareness

> Thinking about yourself as an individual and analyzing your own actions allows you to develop an identity within society and to perceive that identify. Public self-awareness is when you become aware of how you appear to others and private self-awareness is the way you see and conceptualize yourself within your own mind.

7.2 Issues/policies that mutual responsibility supports

Here's a few of the issues/policies that mutual responsibility supports:

- The social safety net: Medicare, Social Security.

- Progressive taxation: The more you benefit from society, the more you should give back so others can benefit.

- Sustainability/Saving the environment.

- Programs to end poverty.

- Investment in jobs.

- Education.

- Cooperation with other countries; worldwide/global initiatives.

- Green energy.

- Aid programs to foreign countries.

- Immigration reform.

Figure 7.1 shows some aspects of taxation within the frame of mutual responsibility.

Within this frame, taxes are the dues that support our union. The basic idea is that the more you benefit from being in our union, the more you should pay back. Without these dues, the union starves and we become a bunch of people endlessly competing with each other.

Basically, we would no longer be a country.

This is not an overstatement but is, in fact, what many organizations want. Typically, these organizations already have their own government and do not want to be a part of the United States. The U.S. Chamber of Commerce could be considered one of these organizations. It has it's own governing structure that will still be around if the United States government is "drowned in the bathtub."

Some churches fall into this category as well; they prefer their own governance to the democracy of the United States.

Mutual responsibility: when you benefit you pay back

Idle wealth taxes

Estate contributions

Corporate taxes

Progressive income taxes

Luxury taxes

Trade taxes/capital gains taxes

Property taxes

Payroll/FICA social security taxes

Sales/consumption taxes

Flat income taxes

Regressive taxes

Voluntary donations

Selfishness: those with the most avoid responsibility

Currently Acceptable

Figure 7.1   Taxation policy options reframed within a mutual responsibility frame.

7.3   How to use the mutual responsibility frame

I've found that mutual responsibility is one of the easiest values to bring up in conversations. This is probably for a couple reasons:

1. It's an extension of individual (or personal) responsibility

2. It has strong roots in most religions

In other words, most people are already somewhat familiar with the concept in some way, shape, or form.

Interestingly enough, corporations promote mutual responsibility but only within the corporation. That is, employees within a corporation are encouraged to trust, collaborate, and respect each other to further company goals. However, strangely enough, their encouragement is limited. Outside of work, we're encouraged to act selfishly.

In discussions, find out who people trust, who they work with, who they cooperate with. This allows you to establish a basis for cooperation. If someone is trying to justify selfishness, find out who, how, and where they cooperate.

Because admit it, no one works alone on everything; it would be impossible. Science would advance at a snail's pace without a scientific community. Commerce would grind to a halt without trust and cooperation. Just about any group you can think of would collapse into a bunch of individuals fighting each other without trust and mutual responsibility.

After people start to realize they don't operate in a vacuum, it starts to become easier to see that corporate lobbyists are only interested in telling others not to cooperate because it advances one of their top priorities: cheap labor.

One of my favorite Internet quotes on the topic:

> There are 12 cookies sitting on a table. The rich take 11 leaving only a single cookie. Then they turn to the Tea Party and say "Those unions are trying to take your cookie."

In other words, why is it OK for people to cooperate and work together within a corporation or as a group of corporations (such as the U.S. Chamber of Commerce) but whenever people get together to cooperate, its "socialism"?

Questions to ask:

- Are you responsible for your family? For relatives? For your neighbor? Others in our country? Others around the world?

- Who do you collaborate with at work?

- Why isn't it OK for people to organize as a union? Shouldn't people have this freedom?

- What happens if lightning strikes someone's house and it burns down? (The concept of insurance is based on mutual responsibility.)

Use your own best judgment to gauge where people are in terms of their understanding of mutual responsibility and ask questions as appropriate.

The point is that corporate special interest groups are trying to erase this belief when it comes to communities and organizations that either a) threaten them (government, unions), or b) they could exploit for more profit if privatized (public schools, parks, water, public airwaves, natural resources).

Why is it acceptable for people to act in their own self-interests when it comes to making purchases, but not to act in their self-interests when it comes to bargaining with employers?

7.4   Example: The tragedy of the commons

Target: Reasonable people who have bought into the argument that self-interest always leads to a greater good.
Goal: Demonstrate scenarios where people acting in their own self-interest leads to the worst possible outcome.

Ayn Rand is a curious character.

If you haven't heard of Rand, I'd suggest a quick overview of *The Virtue of Selfishness*. Don't pay for it, but find a library copy or read a synopsis online. The reason I suggest this is that much of her thinking is at the heart of corporate special interest propaganda.

Figure 7.2   Ayn Rand Institute. [Fit09]

Alan Greenspan was a member of Rand's inner circle in the 1950s and 1960s and contributed several essays to her book *Capitalism: The Unknown Ideal*. Ron Paul, as you know, is a fan, going so far as to name his son after Rand. Ronald Reagan wrote in a personal letter, "Am an admirer of Ayn Rand." [Lev11]

A few other notable Randians include: Paul Ryan (R-WI), Farrah Fawcett, Glenn Beck, Hugh Hefner, Rush Limbaugh, U.S. Supreme Court Justice Clarence Thomas, and former South Carolina governor Mark Sanford.

Many others don't talk about Ayn Rand in public because her ideas are too radical but you will see her beliefs on display when people talk about "free markets," selfishness, and staying out of the way of markets. In Rand's world, business owners are superheroes fighting the evil of those out to perform good.

The belief, for example, that the pursuit of self-interest always leads to a greater good is more Ayn Rand than Adam Smith, more religious belief than economic principle.

Rand's belief in extreme self-interest is summed up by this quote from a 1960 lecture she delivered at Yale, Brooklyn College, and Columbia University:

> If any civilization is to survive, it is the morality of altruism that men
> have to reject.
> —Ayn Rand,1960. [Ran60]

In her view, there is only self-interest and altruism and the latter should always be rejected.

I consider her curious (others might say cultish) because of the extreme dichotomy at the heart of her philosophy: only self-interest or altruism. Only freedom or slavery. Only good or evil.

Sound familiar?

Compare this to Hillel's philosophy of balance between self-interest and community.

This is why, however, when speaking with people who have read or believe in Rand, you may get extreme reactions. Literally, any sign of caring about others, in Rand's worldview, is weakness.

When I encounter this conceptual framework, I contest the frame that individual self-interest always leads to a greater good and establish a better frame of mutual responsibility.

One way to do this is over a beer with a couple of napkins using the classic "prisoner's dilemma" problem from game theory to illustrate the tragedy of the commons [Pou92].

Before beginning, you may want to place a bet with your friend. Something like: "I bet I can prove to you that acting out of self-interest doesn't always lead to the best outcome."

Here's how to set up the prisoner's dilemma:

> You and your buddy rob a bank. You're pretty good, but you get caught. Fortunately, you hid the money. You're in separate jail cells. One day the D.A. comes in and tells you, I want to make you a deal. If you confess to the crime and implicate your buddy, I'll ask for a pardon. If you don't, I'm gonna ask for 10 years. Oh, and by the way, I'm making this same deal to your buddy. If he confesses and you don't, he gets to go free and you get 10 years in prison. If you both confess, you'll both get 5 years.

What would you do?

Give your friend a chance to think about it and respond. You may want to prod with advice about acting in his or her own self-interest such as: Remember, if you keep quiet and he confesses, you get 10 years and he goes free.

Figure 7.3 illustrates the options.

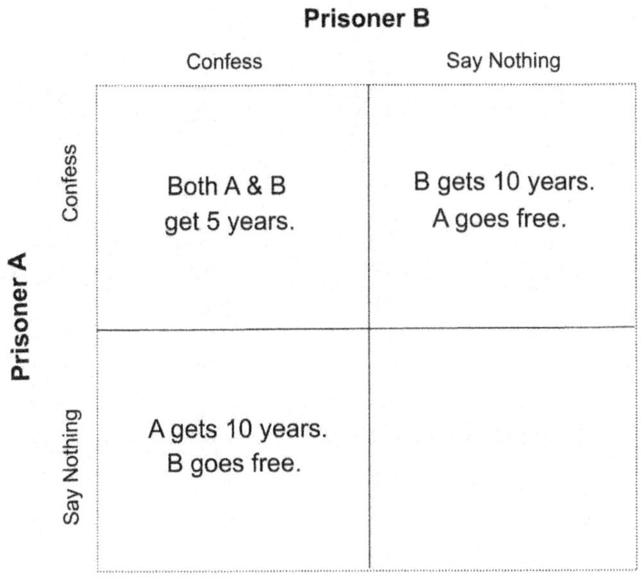

Figure 7.3   Setup for the prisoner's dilemma.

After getting a response, discuss how the most rational move for each (acting out of self-interest) is to both confess. Why?

Because if you confess, you know you'll either go free or get 5 years in jail. If you stay quiet, you risk 10 years.

After you have some fun getting your friend to think about the issue you can fill in the full picture: the D.A. needed confessions for a conviction. If neither person confessed, the D.A. wouldn't be able to get a conviction and you both would have gotten only 1 year on a lesser charge.

The point is that this is an example where acting out of self-interest produces poor results.

Acting out of self-interest, you achieve only the 2nd best outcome—5 years for both. The best outcome would be if you acted in your mutual interest and kept quiet, risking the possibility of going to jail for 10 years. If this were the case, both of you would get only 1 year on a lesser charge.

The full picture is shown in Figure 7.4.

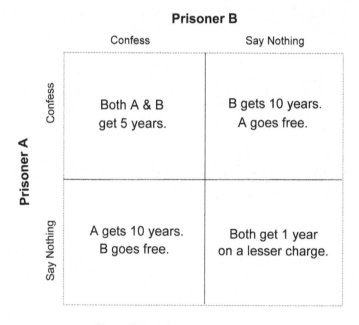

Figure 7.4   The prisoner's dilemma.

Of course, self-interest is enticing. That's the dilemma. If both prisoners knew they would get only 1 year if they cooperated, they'd cooperate.

You can relate the prisoner's dilemma to the classic economic problem: the tragedy of the commons.

The tragedy of the commons is a situation where people acting in their own rational self-interests, act against everyone's long-term interest by depleting a vital resource (sometimes necessary for survival) [Har68].

The issue is, how do you share resources in a sustainable fashion? Take fishing the oceans, for example.

The rational, short-term thing for any individual fisherman to do would be to fish as much as possible. However, the result could lead to overfishing and depletion or even extinction. If this happened, all fishermen could be put out of business.

Other examples include: oceans, rivers, oil (energy), overfishing, the atmosphere, public roads, forests, and the planet itself.

Some of these challenges and our response will likely define the 21st century. Selfishness alone is not the answer. In all likelihood, we're going to need to see cooperation on a scale we've never seen before or new kinds of cooperation we haven't thought of yet. This is the reason mutual responsibility is such a critical core value.

PRACTICE

7.1   What are some areas of your life where you've acted selfishly? What are some areas where you've acted to help other people or other people have helped you?

7.2   Where would you start if someone believed that selfishness always produced a greater good?

7.3   Ask someone you know about the groups they belong to outside of work (that is, sports, family, clubs, trade associations, churches, community groups, and so on). How do they contribute to these groups? Do they feel responsible for helping others in the group?

7.4   Share your conversation about **mutual responsibility** with a friend or blog about it online (at a site like *Daily Kos* or other political forum).

CHAPTER 8

FRAME 4: EQUALITY

> In truth, laws are always useful to those with possessions and harmful to those who have nothing; from which it follows that the social state is advantageous to men only when all possess something and none has too much.
> —Jean-Jacques Rousseau, *The Social Contract*. [Rou02]

In my experience, the equality frame is the frame people are most familiar with, whether they agree with it or disagree with it.

We're familiar with the equality frame in large part because of the civil rights movement, the women's rights movement, the gay rights movement, and the more recent marriage equality movement.

And also from founding documents like *The Declaration of Independence*:

> We hold these truths to be self-evident, that all men are created equal.

Though it took a while for this to be true for women and the slaves in our country, this foundational building block was eventually interpreted correctly as: "all people are created equal."

The phrase in some form or another has been adopted in constitutions around the world over. Here is a more modern version from the United Nations Declaration of Human Rights [UN14]:

> All human beings are born free and equal in dignity and rights.

You know this frame.

The equality frame is also tremendously important even in business because of the idea that there should be a level playing field, that no company should somehow have an unfair advantage. According to this value, there should be competition, but the competition should be fair and must take place within certain guidelines.

8.1   Aspects of equality

Because most people know this frame well and are comfortable using it, I'm going to assume a much greater comfort level and focus on a few areas which might not be as familiar.

First though, some of the components of the equality frame:

Equality of opportunity

> There are many debated definitions of equal opportunity but the basic idea is that everyone should have a fair shot in life. Circumstances shouldn't be too skewed in the favor of any single race, ethnicity, religion, class, sexual orientation, sex, class, or age. The principle behind equality of opportunity is fairness. Another way to think about this is that everyone starts from the same place, no one should start from a particularly advantageous standpoint. Equality of opportunity is linked to the idea that people should be judged on what they become and want to be, rather than the situation into which they were born. That is, identify is up to the individual.

Equality before the law

> Everyone is equal before the law and no one is above the law. Everyone is entitled to due process and fairness before the law. Everyone is entitled to equal protection of the law.

Equal rights

- All people should be treated as equals and have the same political, economic, social, and civil rights.

- All people have the same fundamental worth and social status. We live in a horizontal society, not a caste society in terms of social rank.

Fair outcome

This is often referred to as *equality of outcome*. While equality of opportunity generally concerns itself more with where people start or where they begin, equality of outcome is concerned with results. Once again, there are many debates around the idea, even more so than equality of opportunity. Where I think most people would agree from a moral standpoint is that there should be a reasonable range of economic outcomes. That is, if all of the benefits of a system went to only a few people, this system would be viewed as morally corrupt. I personally find the term equality of outcome itself problematic as it sounds like the desirable goal is the straw man of everyone having an exactly equal outcome. I believe more moral common ground can be found for the idea that people should receive fair compensation for their contributions and work. In other words, that inequality shouldn't be too great—is there really a difference of a million between a person with $10,000 wealth as a person with $1 billion wealth?

Once again, there are likely other aspects of equality. These listed here are the aspects I've found most useful in conversations.

8.2 Issues/policies that equality supports

Some of the policies and issues that equality supports:

- Equal rights
  - Civil rights
  - Lesbian, Gay, Bisexual, and Transgender (LGBT) rights
  - Women's rights
- Voting rights
- Marriage equality
- Democracy

- Equality in the marketplace

- Fair pay

- A living wage

- A progressive tax code:

  – Estate taxes

  – Luxury taxes

  – Corporate taxes

  – Idle wealth taxes

Figure 8.1 shows some aspects of voting within the frame of equality.

Within this frame, everyone should have equal opportunity and access to the ballot box regardless of race, gender, job, or sexual orientation. If we limit the rights of some people to vote, they are not equal participants in our democracy.

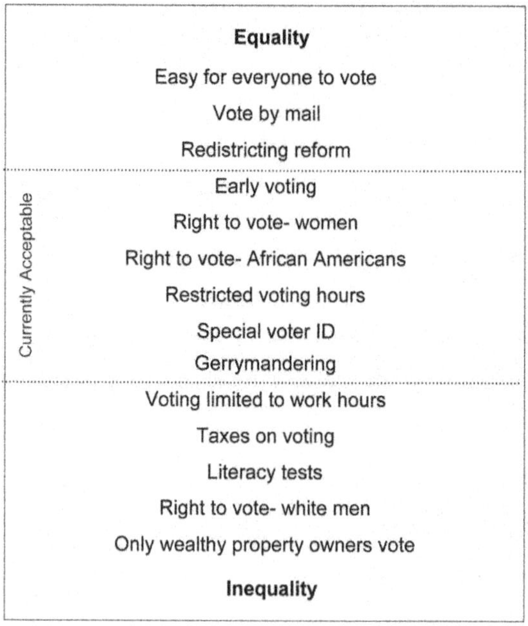

Equality

Easy for everyone to vote

Vote by mail

Redistricting reform

Early voting

Right to vote- women

Right to vote- African Americans

Restricted voting hours

Special voter ID

Gerrymandering

Voting limited to work hours

Taxes on voting

Literacy tests

Right to vote- white men

Only wealthy property owners vote

Inequality

Currently Acceptable

Figure 8.1   Voting options within the frame of equality.

Voting could also easily be framed within the context of democracy. The important thing to realize is that within a big government/small government frame it's not hard to think that we should maximize efficiency by spending as little on the voting process as possible. If we value democracy and equality, however, this becomes absurd.

8.3   How to use the equality frame

Because most people I've spoken with understand how to use the equality frame to talk about social issues, I'm going to focus on a few ways to use **equality** in economic conversations.

The work of Thomas Piketty has demonstrated that the rate of return on capital (basically, return on wealth) is typically higher than the rate of growth of income and output. Basically, what this means is that over time, the rich will get richer and wealth will accumulate in the hands of a few.

Another way of thinking about this is that Piketty's work provides empirical data to back up the old saying that "It takes money to make money."

Piketty argues that eventually market economies will eventually become dominated by those lucky enough to have inherited wealth.

Why we haven't noticed this trend before, Piketty argues, is that the tyranny of inherited wealth was destroyed by two world wars in the 20th century [Ygl14]. In other words, in the 20th century, two world wars flipped the Monopoly board and reset the game.

Another reason this may not have been noticed as much in the United States is the relative age of our country. In other words, at the onset of our country, wealth in the form of land was often available to anyone who simply wanted it and was willing to move West. In many ways, because we were such a young country, we were a country of more equal opportunity with resources widely available to those who simply wanted them to start a better life.

These conditions no longer hold true and over time, as Piketty's data demonstrate, the rate of growth of capital has reasserted itself even in America and will likely continue through the 21th century.

Keep in mind we're not talking about the kind of inequality between a doctor and a baker. This is the difference between the wealth of a Walton and an average person.

This snowball effect of wealth leads to:

- Increased corruption

  - Societies with high inequality tend to adopt policies that hinder long-term growth due to conflicts between the holders of economic power and political power [Ber11].

- Decreased mobility

- Destruction of the middle class

- Increased social instability as people struggle just to make ends meet

Piketty's work provides convincing data for a need to focus more on equality of outcome: Is the system we have producing a broader prosperity? Do we have a working economy?

Christopher Hayes argues [Hay12]:

> The two [equality of opportunity and outcome] aren't so neatly separated. If you don't concern yourself at all with equality of outcomes, you will, over time, produce a system with horrendous equality of opportunity. This is the paradox of meritocracy: It can only truly flower in a society that starts out with a relatively high degree of equality.

The moral of this story, if we want a meritocracy, we need to work for fairer outcomes from our economic system. If we want a society that values upward mobility and earned income over inherited wealth, greater economic equality needs to be a component of a working economy.

What I've found in conversations where things get to be a bit tricky is that most in the United States (with the exception of the Millennial generation) have grown up in a society that started at a much more equal point with much greater opportunity. They therefore often don't see the effects of accumulated wealth and disproportionate economic inequality on our society.

In discussions with people born before the mid-1980s, it's often easier to talk with them about their children and making sure similar economic opportunities exist. With Millennials, the conversation is much simpler as their experiences have been vastly different from those of their parents and generations before them.

Often, Millennials have done everything right in life, followed all the rules, taken out loans to get a good education, built up their resumes, worked hard, and it still isn't enough. It's easier to explain that working harder isn't the answer to people who are working hard and getting nowhere than it is to people who have worked hard and benefited simply because of *when* they were born.

8.4 Questions to ask

- Is there more opportunity now than 10 years ago? 20 years ago?
- Do people who work deserve to share in the profits? Should wages increase with productivity? Or should all the benefit go to owners?
- How does income inequality affect democracy?
- Would you want to live on an island where one person owned the entire island?
- Do markets reflect conditions of inequality rather than fix them?
  - Lower women's wages
  - Skill/wage gaps by race
  - Perpetuation of wealth and class
- Did markets fix _____?
  - Slavery
  - The right to vote for women
  - Child labor
- Will a shrinking middle class impact economic demand?

8.5 Example: The game of Monopoly and discussions about wealth

Target: People interested in laissez-faire economics.
Goal: Illustrate how the economy works best when money is relatively evenly distributed.

The game of Monopoly is a rather interesting lesson in laissez-faire capitalism. It teaches that investing in properties and developing those properties is the way to win the economic game.

There are also several interesting moral principles that the game teaches:

1. **It's not always about skill:** Even if you play the game to the best of your ability, a roll of the dice could determine whether you ever have the opportunity to gain a monopoly of properties. Assuming everyone understands the basic capitalist principles and plays the same way, it comes down to luck.

2. **The rich get richer:** After you make a little money, its easy to leverage that money to make trades and develop properties further. Meanwhile, after all the properties are purchased, those without quickly become poor.

3. **Wealth, once entrenched, changes little:** After the properties are distributed to those in the game, very little acts to change the dynamic of the rich getting richer and the poor getting poorer. In fact, if you own no property and everyone else does, the best place to land is in jail.

4. **The rules disproportionally impact those at the bottom:** Small fines and going to jail don't really matter if you're the owner of the monopolies.

The game of Monopoly makes an excellent example to use in discussions because everyone knows the game.

To begin, ask people if they've ever played Monopoly. What happens? How is that different or similar to our economy?

Here are a few notes:

- In Monopoly, everyone starts out with roughly the same odds of winning. In reality, all of us were born with the game already in progress and most of the properties already owned. Most of the monopolies have already been built.

- It's fun at first to play Monopoly when everyone has an equal shot. This is the promise of equal opportunity in America. However, a select few of us are born to the owners of large Boardwalk and Park Place developments. Most of us are born to the owners of a house on a property like Tennessee Ave.

- The game is designed to produce winners and losers. After playing for a while, it's designed to quickly shift wealth upwards. This is similar to Thomas Piketty's findings that the rate of return on capital exceeds the rate of growth for income and growth. People don't make as much income passing *Go* as they do from owning properties. Wealth accumulates and concentrates with the owners.

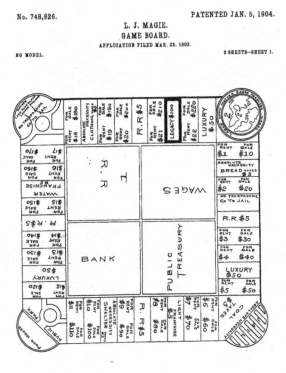

Figure 8.2   Patent submission drawing for *The Renter's Game*, 1904. [Mag04]

- Why then don't the rich own everything in our society? It's getting closer to a point where they do. But there were some safeguards put in place to free up wealth. These include the progressive income tax, the estate tax, corporate taxes, and luxury taxes. These taxes take a portion from someone who has built up a monopoly and puts it back into the public pool. Wealth circulates again and can be earned or used for the public good.

- If money primarily flows in one direction, upwards, this leads to stagnation and an economy where newcomers have few resources available to them and little room to grow or start their own businesses.

At first, Monopoly is fun to play. Everyone competes relatively equally and on equal footing. Eventually, however, one person owns everything and it's no longer fun unless you're that one person. Everyone but the person winning prays they won't land on an owned property.

Think back in our history to the colonization of America. Resources were open to anyone willing to move West. This was how *The Homestead Act of 1862* worked; land was given away to anyone willing to move West of the Mississippi. Similar to the start of a Monopoly game, everyone had resources to achieve their dreams. Of course there were flaws with this idea (see American Indians, removal of) but the availability of resources, such as land to the average American, likely blunted the impacts of accumulated wealth in America during the 18th and 19th centuries.

During the 20th century the affects of accumulation were blunted because two world wars reset the game. Also, to end the Great Depression, significant taxes on idle wealth were put in place in America so that this money would once again serve the public good. Government spending on the public good is another way to offset inequality. Piketty takes this a step further by arguing for a global tax on wealth [Pik14].

As the 21st century opens, we're seeing wealth accumulating at the top and staying there. It is used to produce more wealth. Or to protect wealth with propaganda and police. Or to lobby government for favorable legislation to create more wealth. These conditions lead to economic and political stagnation and the perpetuation of established monopolies like the oil industry.

8.6 Example: The case for equal regulations

> **Target:** Business people who understand the need for a level playing field, but argue that deregulation as the only answer.
>
> **Goal:** Introduce a new solution, one that most people don't think of when it comes to regulation.

The U.S. Chamber of Commerce lobbies extensively against regulations, especially when it comes to regulations on the energy industry.

To find their latest argument, I had to look no further than the title of an editorial in today's news [Mcc14]: "EPA's new plan to target greenhouse gases will kill jobs, devastate middle class."

According to the editorial:

> These regulations are a lose-lose proposition all around for U.S. jobs, for families, for the U.S. economy, for our nation's competitiveness overseas, and for those who want to see a reduction in global carbon emissions.

Stepping back from all the fear and hyperbolic spin, are there valid economic arguments against regulation?

The argument I've heard most often is the level playing field argument. You hear this above when the author talks about "our nation's competitiveness overseas." This is what some of our largest businesses truly fear, that a competitor overseas will have a competitive edge because of lower regulations.

The argument is always to reduce regulations.

What rarely gets mentioned is that reducing regulations is really just a special case of a level playing field. It's the special case where there are no regulations and industries supposedly regulate themselves (which we know doesn't really happen).

We could also level the playing field by raising regulations overseas or levying an additional tax on overseas companies who fail to meet certain standards. This would also equalize competition and it would do it in a manner where we receive all the benefits of the regulations: a cleaner environment, safer workplace, less exploitation of workers, and so on.

In other words, there are other options.

The U.S. Chamber of Commerce, however, tries to keep these options out of the conversation because they are pursuing the path of least resistance for their clients.

Unfortunately, the quest to lower regulations is much like the quest for lower taxes, one of the best lobbying tactics is to find someplace else with lower regulations and threaten to leave if the United States doesn't lower its regulations. And if the United States does lower regulations, try to put pressure on another country to lower their regulations even further.

This is a classic race to the bottom situation where discussion of any public good is shoved to the side.

Wouldn't a better situation be to collaborate internationally to set standards to raise the bar for all people? The United States used to be a leader when it came to the environment. Wouldn't a better situation be to fight to bring other countries up to our standards (or former standards)?

The way to frame this is to talk about equal regulations or a level playing field.

PRACTICE

8.1   What aspects of equality are important to you?

8.2   Has there ever been a situation where you felt you were treated unfairly? Why?

8.3   What problems can you think of that result from inequality?

8.4   How would you talk about inequality with someone who states a version of the belief "life isn't fair, there will always be inequality"?

CHAPTER 9

FRAME 5: FREEDOM

Why can't you tell knock-knock jokes about America?
Because freedom rings.

—Unknown

Freedom.

What do you think of when you hear this word?

Naomi Wolf, writing about the dangers of the National Defense Authorization Act (NDAA), wrote: "As one of my Facebook community members remarked bitterly, of our House representatives, our Senate leaders, and our president, 'They hate our freedoms.'" [Wol12]

Figure 9.1   Rock flag eagle! t-shirt, *It's Always Sunny in Philadelphia.*

This is a joke I've made before (and you may very well have too) in the voice of a Duck Dynasty conservative talking about liberals: "Why do they hate our free-dums?"

I believe the word freedom has become something of a distasteful word because, by and large, the term is being redefined by corporate lobbyists and media to mean "freedom of capital" or "freedom of individual spending choices."

In his book *Freedom*, Jonathan Franzen wrote [Fra10]:

> I think the iPod is the true face of Republican politics, and I'm in favor of the music industry really getting out in front on this one, and becoming more active politically, and standing up proud and saying it out loud: We in the Chiclet-manufacturing business are not about social justice, we're not about accurate or objectively verifiable information, we're not about meaningful labor, we're not about a coherent set of national ideals, we're not about wisdom. We're about choosing what WE want to listen to and ignoring everything else. ... We're about giving ourselves a mindless feel-good treat every five minutes. We're about the relentless enforcement and exploitation of our intellectual-property rights. We're about persuading ten-year-old children to spend twenty-five dollars on a cool little silicone iPod case that costs a licensed Apple Computer subsidiary thirty-nine cents to manufacture.

Corporate special interest groups have redefined "freedom" as "selfishness."

Like Wolf's Facebook friend and Franzen, we should be outraged about this narrow definition. Unfortunately, in our outrage, we often stop at pointing out the misuse of "freedom" instead of helping others understand what freedom means to us.

If we stick to the standard right/left script where conservatives define what freedom means (the freedom to make spending decisions) and liberals joke about their beliefs, we win over no one and risk losing the freedoms we often take for granted.

When I speak about what freedom means to me, I've found that most people I know, even conservatives, share many of the same values. We only realize this, however, if we stop playing the right/left game long enough to talk about it.

9.1 Aspects of freedom

George Lakoff wrote an entire book on the frame of freedom (*Whose Freedom?: The Battle Over America's Most Important Idea*) that is well worth the read.

Here, I'll highlight in my own words a few aspects that I've found most useful. Likely, many of these will sound familiar:

Individual freedom—The pursuit of goals and dreams

> At its very heart, freedom is the ability to pursue your goals, basically, the American dream of life, liberty, and the pursuit of happiness.

Freedom for others

> - The exercise of your freedom should not interfere with the freedom of others. That is, you're not "free" to assault people. This is why there are laws and rules. This is why freedom is more than selfishness.
>
> - Think of a traffic system and the rules and regulations that allow traffic to flow freely without injury/harm.
>
> - We are most "free" when everyone acts positively to maximize the freedom of others.

Freedom is dynamic

> Throughout the years we've successfully expanded freedom in some of the following ways: civil rights, voting rights, property rights, tol-

erance, education, science, public health, workers' rights, and infrastructure we've developed for the common good: universities, banking, the Internet, social services, transportation, science.

Economic freedom

- The freedom to earn a living for you and your family. This requires the ability to fairly bargain for wages both individually and as groups (to equalize negotiating power).

- Economic freedom is also hurt in the case of illness or accident. Your ability to work is threatened. This is why access to health care has always been so important to economic freedom. This is also why Social Security is important as you grow older—it provides economic freedom when you can no longer work.

Freedom of religion

- The freedom to practice any religion so long as it doesn't interfere with the freedom of others or override the democratic laws of the land.

- The separation of church and state. The government shouldn't establish a state religion or favor any one particular religion over another.

- Freedom of religion also means freedom from religion, meaning no one can force individuals to join a specific religion.

Of course this is limited, but I've found that these aspects make a nice start.

9.2   Issues/policies that freedom supports

To give you an idea why freedom as a concept is so important, here are some of the issues it supports:

- Investment in infrastructure

- A living wage

- Academic tenure

- NSA reform

- Public schools

- Health care as a right

- Separation of church and state

- Reducing income inequality

- Civil liberties

- Net neutrality

- Social safety net policies (Medicare, Social Security, unemployment benefits)

- Voting rights

- Immigration reform

- Social justice and equality

Freedom of religion was hugely important to our founding fathers. In their view, religious freedom was as much about freedom from religion as it was freedom to practice religion.

Figure 9.1 shows some aspects of religion within the frame of freedom.

Most Freedom

Constitutional amendment: separation of church and state

Laws are agnostic

Religions not supported with public funds

Separation of church and state

Ability to choose and practice any religion

Freedom to leave a religion

Religious pluralism

Freedom from religion

Laws subject to religious "harm" test

Currently Acceptable

Religions able to "opt out" of democratic laws

Religious laws supercede democractic laws

Religious government

Persecution of "non-supported" religions

Least Freedom

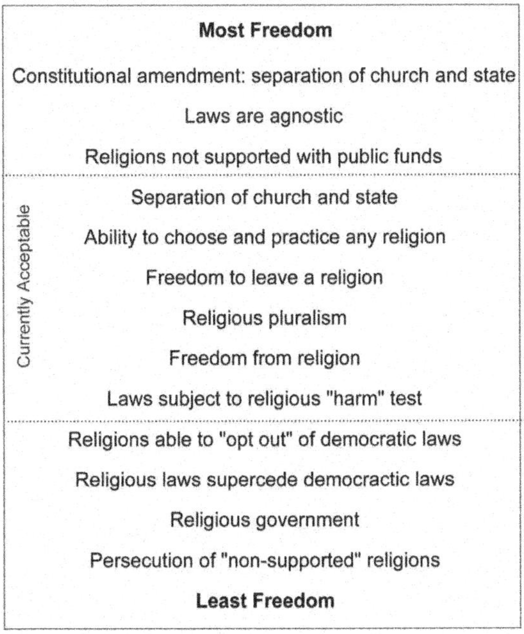

Figure 9.2   Religion within the frame of freedom.

The *Virginia Statute for Religious Freedom* written by Thomas Jefferson proclaimed:

> Be it enacted by General Assembly that no man shall be compelled to frequent or support any religious worship, place, or ministry whatsoever, nor shall be enforced, restrained, molested, or burthened in his body or goods, nor shall otherwise suffer, on account of his religious opinions or belief; but that all men shall be free to profess, and by argument to maintain, their opinions in matters of religion, and that the same shall in no wise diminish, enlarge, or affect their civil capacities.

These sentiments found their way into the Constitution as the First Amendment to the Bill of Rights:

> Congress shall make no law respecting an establishment of religion, or prohibiting the free exercise thereof ...

Various religious and corporate special interest groups have been trying to redefine the concept of freedom in order to benefit their respective groups.

A corporate definition of freedom looks more like consumer choice. A religious definition of freedom looks like the freedom of a particular religion from United States law.

9.3   How to use the freedom frame

In my conversations, I've found that freedom is often brought up in a very limited sense: freedom from government or 'free" markets.

This is a direct result of corporate marketing tactics designed to redefine "freedom" as the ability to make consumer choices. Capital (and the power that goes with it) should be free to acquire more capital and your freedom is limited to what you own. The way this belief is often sold to us is that a greater good will happen when markets are "freed."

You will hear this belief a great deal because many people have bought into it. Especially people who grew up during a time when resources and opportunities were readily available.

Whenever freedom is brought up, you have an opportunity. The opportunity is to expand on this very limited definition of freedom.

In other words, when freedom as a subject comes up, rather than mock someone's view, use it as an opportunity to talk about what freedom means to you.

Use it as an opportunity to expand the corporate-limited definition of freedom.

9.3.1 Some questions to ask

Winston Churchill asked a number of important questions about freedom in *The Second World War vol. 2: Triumph and Tragedy*. In this work, Churchill asks the question, "What is freedom?"

He then lists a series of questions to ask to determine if a society is free. I first read these courtesy of *Daily Kos* author Anakai [Ana14]:

1. Is there the right to free expression of opinion and of opposition and criticism of the government of the day?

2. Have the people the right to turn out a government of which they disapprove, and are constitutional means provided by which they can make their will apparent?

3. Are their courts of justice free from violence by the executive and from threats of mob violence, and free of all association with particular political parties?

4. Will these courts administer open and well-established laws which are associated in the human mind with the broad principles of decency and justice?

5. Will there be fair play for poor as well as for rich, for private persons as well as government officials?

6. Will the rights of the individual, subject to his duties to the state, be maintained and asserted and exalted?

7. Is the ordinary peasant or workman who is earning a living by daily toil and striving to bring up a family free from the fear that some grim police organization under the control of a single party, like the Gestapo, started by the Nazi and Fascist parties, will tap him on the shoulder and pack him off without fair or open trial to bondage or ill treatment?

A few additional questions:

- How free are you if you have to work three jobs?

- What do people need to best pursue their goals in life? Education? Infrastructure? Teachers? Resources? Money?

- What happens when those who have benefited the most from our country decide they want to keep all the benefits for themselves?

- How is opportunity different for the wealthy, for the middle class, and for the poor?

- Which is more important, free people or free markets?

9.3.2   The Commonwealth as freedom enabler

Government is so demonized that we often forget that one of the founding ideas of our country was the idea of the common good to enable freedom and the pursuit of individual goals.

This utilitarian idea informed the early commonwealth governments of Massachusetts and Virginia. From the Constitution of the Commonwealth of Massachusetts:

> The body politic is formed by a voluntary association of individuals: it is a social compact, by which the whole people covenants with each citizen, and each citizen with the whole people, that all shall be governed by certain laws for the common good.

The idea of a common good is echoed in the Declaration of Independence:

- We have "certain unalienable Rights, that among these are Life, Liberty and the pursuit of Happiness. That to secure these rights, Governments are instituted among Men, deriving their just powers from the consent of the governed."

- "He [the king] has refused his Assent to Laws, the most wholesome and necessary for the public good."

And in the Constitution in the form of "general welfare":

- "We the People of the United States, in Order to form a more perfect Union, establish Justice, insure domestic Tranquility, provide for the common defence, promote the general Welfare, and secure the Blessings of Liberty to ourselves and our Posterity, do ordain and establish this Constitution for the United States of America."

- "The Congress shall have Power To lay and collect Taxes, Duties, Imposts and Excises, to pay the Debts and provide for the common Defence and general Welfare of the United States; but all Duties, Imposts and Excises shall be uniform throughout the United States."

Towards this end, throughout our history we've developed a strong infrastructure to support people achieving their goals and the common good. Some aspects of our commonwealth:

- Public education

- National and local parks

- Defense

- National Institute of Health (NIH)

- Roads

- The banking system

- Courts

- The postal system

- Libraries

- Railroads

- The Internet

- Fire and police departments

- Public utilities

- The telephone system

- The Federal Communications Commission (FCC)

- The Securities and Exchange Commission (SEC)

Infrastructure increases the ability of people to pursue their goals in one form or another. Our infrastructure was not-for-profit originally though some aspects have been privatized and others are threatened by privatization.

One thing to consider about privatization is the profit motive and whether it interferes with the goal of the public good.

In health care, for example, health care and health care insurance company incentives lead to some of the highest costs in the world with little impact on overall lifespan. In other words, certain corporate operators were exploiting the system for more profit and gain than they deserved without any significant increase in public benefit. Basically, the market wasn't working.

In communications, as the FCC has come under more and more industry influence, we see more and more consolidation, less choice, and less use of our public airwaves for public uses like education.

The question worth asking (which too often goes unasked) when it comes to privatization, will private efforts still serve a public good? Or, how do we make sure they do?

The argument we so often hear is that markets know best. But, when set up poorly, rather than lead to a better society, markets serve to create only huge windfalls for a select few.

9.4   Example: Freedom from want

> **Target:** People who desire freedom (just about anyone).
>
> **Goal:** Reframe freedom as the ability to pursue happiness because individuals are free from want. Highlight the importance of freedom to democracy.

Franklin D. Roosevelt gave voice to "freedom from want" in 1941 in his *Four Freedoms* speech [Roo41].

Roosevelt saw our country imperiled by Nazi aggression and wanted the United States to abandon post-World War I isolationist policies.

In his words:

> No realistic American can expect from a dictator's peace international generosity, or return of true independence, or world disarmament, or freedom of expression, or freedom of religion—or even good business.

Towards this end he articulated four essential freedoms as the cornerstones of democracy. Freedom of speech and religion we know about. Freedom from fear was a worldwide reduction in arms to the point where "no nation would be in a position to commit an act of physical aggression against any neighbor."

And freedom from want: "Economic understandings which will secure to every nation a healthy peacetime life for its inhabitants—everywhere in the world."

What did Roosevelt mean by these economic understandings?

In the same speech, he articulates what makes a democracy healthy and strong:

Figure 9.3   *Freedom from Want*, Saturday Evening Post. [Roc43]

- Equality of opportunity for youth and for others

- Jobs for those who can work

- Security for those who need it

- The ending of special privilege for the few

Help those in need. If you can work, you work. Pretty straightforward.

How is this in danger?

We are being told by our wealthiest that they simply do not want to pay for those in need anymore. Instead, they want to avoid their responsibility to our country to increase their own estates. Not only that, but they are reestablishing special privileges based on wealth.

Our country is paying for tax cuts (that primarily benefit the wealthy) by cutting programs to provide economic security: Supplemental Nutrition Assistance Program (SNAP) benefits, job programs, pensions, Medicare, and Social Security.

We would do better from a moral standpoint if we spoke about economic freedom when framing these programs instead of a) fighting for individual programs, or b) calling them entitlements, the corporate framing for these programs.

9.5   Example: The right to education

Target: People who desire freedom (just about anyone).
Goal: Link the right to education to freedom.

Many countries, especially those ahead of us in international ranking, have established the right to an education in their laws or constitution [Lur13].

Rather than focusing on freedom and access to a quality education, however, corporate interest groups in the U.S. are more interested in privatizing schools.

The frames they use to do this are "choice" and "freedom." Consumer choice and consumer freedom [Ale14].

Education, by and large, determines future in the United States.

A privatized system would create tiers of service—higher quality schools for those who can afford it, lower quality for poorer students. It would also allow money intended for education to be used for profit.

Do we really want school systems where people pay according to their class in society? Won't this further reduce upward mobility? Won't this limit opportunity and freedom? Won't this create a "pay to play" situation?

We've long taken for granted the right of every person in this country to receive a free quality public education. If we want this to continue, a good step would be to promote freedom of education as a national value; this

Figure 9.4   Privatizing America's Public Schools. [Ben12]

frame would support establishing education as a right through a national law or Constitutional amendment.

Framing public education within the tradition of American freedom would go a long ways towards helping protect public schools from the corporate groups interested in privatization.

9.6   Example: The right to additional freedoms

Target: Just about everyone.
Goal: Expand the concept of rights beyond the Constitution.

The Ninth Amendment to the Constitution states:

The enumeration in the Constitution, of certain rights, shall not be construed to deny or disparage others retained by the people.

Some examples of freedoms we take for granted today:

1. Freedom to live or travel anywhere in the country

2. Freedom to work at any job

3. Freedom to engage equally in economic transactions

4. Freedom to receive a free education in quality public schools

5. Freedom to marry and raise a family

6. The right to privacy—Freedom from intrusion and spying

Yet none of these freedoms is explicitly mentioned in the Constitution. Does this mean we don't have these freedoms?

According to the Ninth Amendment, no.

Yet most of the effort during the past 30 years has been about restricting the notion of freedom, limiting us to only those freedoms strictly enumerated in the Constitution. Oddly enough, this was the same issue which warranted the passage of the Ninth Amendment.

James Madison speaking out against the original Bill of Rights [Mad00]:

> It has been objected also against a bill of rights, that, by enumerating particular exceptions to the grant of power, it would disparage those rights which were not placed in the enumeration; and it might follow, by implication, that those rights which were not singled out, were intended to be assigned into the hands of the General Government, and were consequently insecure.

In other words, just because a right isn't specifically listed in the Constitution, doesn't mean we don't have that right.

This objection led to the inclusion of the Ninth Amendment stating that when forming our government, the people retained rights in addition to those enumerated.

In Griswold vs. Connecticut, where the Supreme Court upheld the use of condoms based on a marital right to privacy, Justice William Douglas said the following as part of the majority opinion [Gri65]:

> To hold that a right so basic and fundamental and so deep-rooted in our society as the right of privacy in marriage may be infringed because that right is not guaranteed in so many words by the first eight amendments to the Constitution is to ignore the Ninth Amendment and to give it no effect whatsoever.

The Constitution does not specify rights we have. The Constitution only specifies that certain rights can't be taken away by government.

In other words, just because it's not in the Bill of Rights, doesn't mean it's not a right. If government is going to try to take away more rights, maybe it's time to put them in the Constitution.

PRACTICE

9.1   How is freedom characterized in the media? How does this relate to your definition of freedom?

9.2   Consider the claims about markets. We've been told that consumer choice and markets always lead to a more desirable outcome. One example where this doesn't seem to be the case is ATM fees. Why, for example, aren't there more banks that feature no ATM fees? Are there other examples you can think of where consumer choice doesn't seem to be making a positive impact?

9.3   Think about someone you know who believes in the limited view of freedom as consumer choice. How could you expand on this view? What examples would you use?

9.4   Find someone online or use the person you were thinking of in #3. See if you can broaden that person's view of freedom in a nonconfrontational way by talking about an example of what freedom means to you.

9.5   Share your conversation about **freedom** with a friend or blog about it online (at a site like *Daily Kos* or other political forum).

PART IV

PLAYING

CHAPTER 10

EXAMPLE: MARKETS ARE THINGS WE CREATE

Once you realize that trickle-down economics does not work, you will see the excessive tax cuts for the rich as what they are—a simple upward redistribution of income, rather than a way to make all of us richer, as we were told.
—Ha-Joon Chang, 2010 [Cha10]

Up to this point, I've included bits and pieces of examples to demonstrate five key frames. Here, I'm including a full conversation to help illustrate how to frame and conceptualize issues with people you know.

This example is a Facebook conversation. Facebook is not the best place for conversations where you're looking to win people over.

Ideally, you want to have these types of discussions one-on-one to take the viewing audience out of the equation. You're much more likely to have a productive conversation with someone in a situation where that person isn't trying to save face or put on a show. In one-on-one situations, there's also much more of an opportunity to communicate nonverbally (most communication is non verbal; more on this subject later).

That said, online conversations have a transcript. You can see exactly what others are saying and I can't "embellish" what I said; you'll see all the warts, including my mistakes.

I am, however, only able to have this conversation online because I'm friends with one of the people in the group. I have an established relationship that I value and I make sure to put this first in any conversation.

This example is a group of nine people who would likely self-identify as Libertarians or Tea Party members. At first, I would recommend easier targets. I wanted to demonstrate, however, how this process is the same even with people who favor radically different conceptual frames from my own.

It's the same regardless of audience.

Because there are many people in this discussion, I'm going to use animal icons to represent the folks in the conversation [Fre14].

10.1   The setup

Rabbit is a friend of mine. She is an engineer who teaches at a local college. She would say her primary concern is freedom and most of her frames have their roots in Ayn Rand, the NRA, and Austrian economists, such as Hayek.

She's often open to different ideas, especially if you can prove them to her. She likes musical groups such as the Residents, the Dead Milkmen, early punk, and Rush. She cares deeply about her daughter and spouse and people close to her.

She posted this comment (Figure 10.1) about Paul Ryan discussing how Republicans need to focus on creating more jobs and lowering the deficit.

In this post, Rabbit also highlights the corporate view on government programs, that they are handouts to the undeserving.

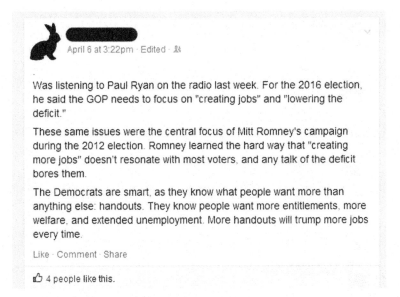

April 6 at 3:22pm · Edited · 👪

Was listening to Paul Ryan on the radio last week. For the 2016 election, he said the GOP needs to focus on "creating jobs" and "lowering the deficit."

These same issues were the central focus of Mitt Romney's campaign during the 2012 election. Romney learned the hard way that "creating more jobs" doesn't resonate with most voters, and any talk of the deficit bores them.

The Democrats are smart, as they know what people want more than anything else: handouts. They know people want more entitlements, more welfare, and extended unemployment. More handouts will trump more jobs every time.

Like · Comment · Share

👍 4 people like this.

Figure 10.1   Rabbit's initial post about Paul Ryan.

10.2   Identify the frames being used

You'll recognize the laissez-faire capitalism frame.

At the center of this frame is a belief that an unregulated market always "does the right thing." Within this frame, you are preventing good if you "interfere" with markets.

Let's explore the frame. Rabbit's friends highlight some of the aspects of the laissez-faire capitalism frame (Figure 10.2).

Other aspects of the laissez-faire capitalism frame include:

- Jobs are created by private individuals and investors.

- Individual initiative made our country great.

- Private industry is more efficient and less wasteful than the public sector.

- Anyone with sufficient self-discipline can succeed.

- People need to have the freedom to make choices within the market.

- Government assistance is a form of "interfering" in markets.

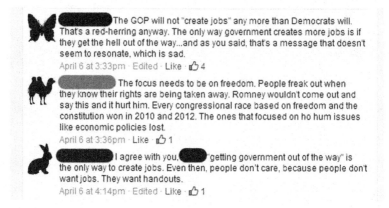

Figure 10.2   Aspects of the laissez-faire capitalism frame.

Figure 10.3   More comments about laissez-faire economics.

You hear this echoed in Butterfly's comment about the government "get[ting] the hell out of the way," Camel's comment about "freedom," and Rabbit's comment about handouts in Figure 10.3.

You also see it in Fish's comment about lazy people who "don't want to sweat for it!!!!" and in Elephant's comment about government infrastructure being a drain on taxpayers.

I think you get the picture. In all likelihood, you could provide plenty more examples.

10.3   Define your goal and what success looks like

Before jumping into any discussion, especially in a public forum like Facebook, decide what you want to get out of the conversation.

Ask yourself: what is my goal?

In this instance, I decided on three goals.

One, not to have the fight turn into the typical right/left, Republican/Democrat back and forth.

Two, to hold the moral high ground. I'll explain more about as the conversation progresses.

And three, to see if I could simply get one or two people to consider something differently. To do this, I'm going to use my own framing of the economy. While this may contain facts and figures and examples, the core is my values and beliefs about a **working economy**.

In a nutshell, I believe that we, the people, design the rules that make markets work. We have the freedom to make the rules any way we choose. We can choose to make these rules so they benefit a tiny few or we can make the rules so they create a broader prosperity.

10.4   Challenge an existing frame

One of the ways I've found effective over the years is to start by challenging the frame with a couple examples that the audience might relate to. I've also found that it's important to challenge the main belief; this is why it's so important to understand the conceptual framing.

Keep the discussion at a values/beliefs level rather than getting into the weeds of any particular policy.

In Figure 10.4, I chose a couple of examples that I felt contradicted the core of the laissez-faire capitalism frame that markets, left to themselves, inherently do good.

Me ⬤⬤⬤ Unfortunately, most of the jobs the private sector has created in the last 15-20 years are low wage jobs in other countries.

From everything I've seen the Paul Ryan/Mitt Romney "jobs" plan looks a lot like "let's make the wages and benefits here look like China".

It's a great plan if you happen to own a corporation or need cheap labor!
April 6 at 9:30pm · Like · 👍 1

Figure 10.4   Challenge an existing frame.

The examples I used are jobs moving overseas and declining wages.

The one "like" that I received on my comment was from my friend, the original poster, Rabbit. I was both pleasantly surprised and not surprised.

It was not surprising because I consider Rabbit to be a very smart person. It was surprising because I hadn't expected her to "like" this comment in a public forum like Facebook.

I made sure in this initial reply to not say anything about the Tea Party or any other name calling. I stuck to what I've observed and what I thought also might be some of the group's frustrations.

From past conversations with similar folks, I know that the focus tends to be on the government and taxes, so I wanted to start shifting the conversation outside of this frame to look at what's going on in the labor market.

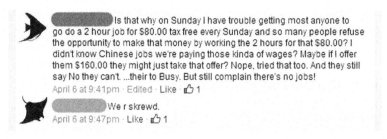

Is that why on Sunday I have trouble getting most anyone to go do a 2 hour job for $80.00 tax free every Sunday and so many people refuse the opportunity to make that money by working the 2 hours for that $80.00? I didn't know Chinese jobs we're paying those kinda of wages? Maybe if I offer them $160.00 they might just take that offer? Nope, tried that too. And they still say No they can't. ...their to Busy. But still complain there's no jobs!
April 6 at 9:41pm · Edited · Like · 👍 1

We r skrewd.
April 6 at 9:47pm · Like · 👍 1

Figure 10.5   An argument I hadn't expected.

Fish responded back first with an argument I hadn't expected (Figure 10.5).

He claimed he couldn't get someone to work for 2 hours for him on Sunday for $40 an hour.

To give him credit for a second, Fish does a great job bringing his own personal experience into the discussion. Personal experience is extremely

Figure 10.6 Fish's view on workers.

convincing because not only is it firsthand but it also takes the shape of a story or narrative used to back up beliefs and values.

Fish goes on to elaborate on the problems he's facing trying to find good workers (Figure 10.6). In his story, he is the hero and his workers are lazy freeloaders.

Now because I don't know Fish personally, I have no way of knowing how Fish conducts his business or who works for him and what they think of him. If I had to guess, my guess would be that many of Fish's challenges are of his own making because he doesn't strike me as a person who would make a good leader.

While I can speculate about Fish's business, however, I have no evidence for this claim other than his behavior online and even if I did have evidence bringing it up likely wouldn't help me with either my goal of getting him to consider something in a different way or with my goal of holding the moral high ground.

So I spoke from my experience and said I never had any trouble finding qualified people for $40 an hour (Figure 10.7).

When you respond from your experience, you make a stronger case than simply rebutting someone else's argument. In my experience, I've never had any trouble finding good people for $40 an hour. Perhaps in some

Me ⬤⬤⬤⬤ I don't have trouble finding people to work for $40 an hour.
Perhaps it's something other than the money ...
April 6 at 10:15pm · Like

Figure 10.7   My experience hiring people.

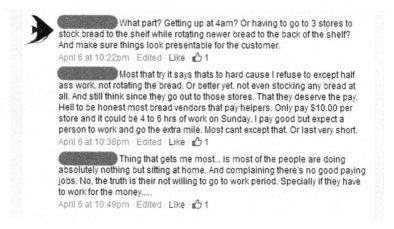

⬤⬤⬤⬤ What part? Getting up at 4am? Or having to go to 3 stores to
stock bread to the shelf while rotating newer bread to the back of the shelf?
And make sure things look presentable for the customer.
April 6 at 10:22pm · Edited · Like · 👍 1

⬤⬤⬤⬤ Most that try it says thats to hard cause I refuse to except half
ass work. not rotating the bread. Or better yet. not even stocking any bread at
all. And still think since they go out to those stores. That they deserve the pay.
Hell to be honest most bread vendors that pay helpers. Only pay $10.00 per
store and it could be 4 to 6 hrs of work on Sunday. I pay good but expect a
person to work and go the extra mile. Most cant except that. Or last very short.
April 6 at 10:38pm · Edited · Like · 👍 1

⬤⬤⬤⬤ Thing that gets me most... is most of the people are doing
absolutely nothing but sitting at home. And complaining there's no good paying
jobs. No, the truth is their not willing to go to work period. Specially if they have
to work for the money.....
April 6 at 10:49pm · Edited · Like · 👍 1

Figure 10.8   Those lazy people who don't want to work.

niche fields like nuclear engineering, but not in food service or retail as
Fish claims.

Fish responded sincerely with some anger apparently directed towards his
employees (Figure 10.8).

To me, one of the interesting things here is how Fish takes his anger at his
personal situation and directs it towards others.

It's also not lost on me that some of his frustration may be race related. I
don't mention any of this, however, because it wouldn't help with any of
my goals of getting people to see a different picture of the economy.

Rabbit and Elephant hop on the lazy people wagon (Figure 10.9).

They really have some strong feelings that poor people are poor because
they choose to be poor.

Rabbit introduces her theory that people aren't working because they can
make more by not working than by working. Elephant brings up a lazy
union worker who brags about how he can't be fired.

"Poor people do things poorly."
April 7 at 6:25am · Like · 👍 1

People will moan & complain nonstop about being poor. But when you offer them a job, they will say they can't do the work; they will complain about the hours, or that it "doesn't pay enough." They will also claim they have a physical or mental condition/disease that prevents them from working.

The real reason is because someone is paying them NOT to work. Why should they work when someone is paying them not to?

If you're earning the equivalent of $12/hour from entitlements, you certainly won't get up every morning and go to work for $12/hour. Heck, you won't even get up and go to work for $20/hour! A lazy person would much rather get $12/hour doing nothing versus $20/hour to work.

So when I need to hire someone, I am competing against the government.
April 7 at 6:35am · Edited · Like · 👍 2

The custodian I mentioned knows how to beat the system and get paid for doing nothing. He sleeps for 4 hours every day in a closet while he is on the clock. He got caught a couple of times. Normally that is grounds for termination, but thanks to his union rep, he got his doctor to write a note saying he is on medication that makes him sleepy, he just dozed off for a minute, and he can't help it because of medical reasons. He has seniority in the union, so they can't get rid of him without getting rid of a lot of others first. He not only knows it, he brags about it. "They can't fire me, ha ha ha", he boasts.
April 7 at 7:22am · Like

Figure 10.9   Poor people "choose" to be poor.

Figure 10.10   What about the people who are like you?

While some of their personal stories may be true, they seem to be extending a few personal experiences into a broad generalization that somehow lazy people are the problem with our economy. This view, of course, is facilitated by corporate radio and TV pundits.

I thought I'd have more success by bringing the conversation back to people who I thought Fish could relate better to, people who were more like him.

I briefly acknowledged Fish's point about people who don't work hard and aren't born rich (Figure 10.10).

My comment may sound a bit harsh but I said it because I too believe in hard work and, outside of winning the lottery or being born rich, I believe our society lacks or is losing the levels of upward mobility we used to enjoy. Not because people aren't working hard enough, though. Still, I can easily agree with the value of hard work.

One of my rules of thumb is to never say anything I don't personally believe. It will sound inauthentic, like John Kerry trying to be pro-gun, or Mitt Romney trying to act like he cares about working people. This rule may sound obvious, but it's harder to do than you think.

I then flipped the conversation back to the hard working people I know.

A newcomer, Turtle, jumped in on the conversation (Figure 10.11) with some ideas about how to incent companies to recreate industry here in the United States.

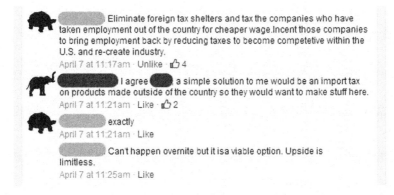

Figure 10.11   Turtle hops on the conversation.

Note that I haven't talked about any solutions. I've focused on personal experiences and have stayed out of any name calling. Subsequently, I haven't been called any names in return.

In many ways, I've already accomplished all three of my goals: 1) The conversation hasn't devolved into name calling or a right/left fight, 2) I've stood up for my beliefs, and 3) I've gotten at least a couple people to start thinking differently.

10.5   Reframe

I thought it worth a shot to push a little further conceptually.

I agreed with Turtle's assessment that current incentives are wrong (Figure 10.12). Again, this is honest agreement. Don't flatter for the sake of flattery. Don't lie. However, when someone says something you believe in, there's no harm and often much help in acknowledging it. The message is, we're more alike than different.

To push further, I brought up "equal regulation," part of the working economy frame. One of the biggest reasons corporations will tell you that they don't like regulations is that they feel it gives competitors in countries with lower regulations an advantage.

We most often hear this argument used conceptually to argue for lower regulations. However, what they're really saying is simply that the playing field isn't level.

Me ⬛⬛⬛ I like where you guys are going. Would like to hear more ideas like this from politicians. I won't argue details but I agree with the idea that current incentives are wrong.

What I also wish we would see is more of an effort to bring other countries up to the standards of the U.S. The argument we typically hear is that we need to get rid of regulations. We hear this argument because our biggest companies feel threatened by countries with few regulations. From a competitive standpoint, less or more regulation doesn't really matter so much though as equal regulation.

April 7 at 11:32am · Like

Figure 10.12   Equal regulation.

You have to analyze WHY it is so much cheaper for work to be performed in India or China versus the U.S.

It is extremely expensive to hire someone in the U.S. In the U.S., the government forces employers to adhere to a myriad of EPA laws, labor laws, unemployment taxes, OSHA laws, insurance, licensing, business taxes, IRS, etc. And then the government tells you that you must compete with countries that do not have an EPA, labor laws, OSHA laws, etc.

Even if you paid your employees NOTHING, you still cannot compete with countries that do not have these laws in place.

April 7 at 11:32am · Edited · Unlike · 👍2

Figure 10.13   Rabbit and I state the same problem.

An equal regulation argument says that instead of creating a race to the bottom and a world with no regulations, we instead should work to raise standards in other countries to level the playing field.

So I pointed out the United States as a standard bearer. We should want other countries to have our environmental and worker protections.

My friend Rabbit posted back almost simultaneously (Figure 10.13).

Interestingly enough, we both brought up the same thing and almost at the same time. I had anticipated his concern that corporations would suffer competitively to corporations in countries with lower regulations.

When you both can at least agree on the same problem, it's a good sign.

10.6   Give credit where credit is due

So I gave her credit in Figure 10.14.

Me Hahahahah ... well said, . You hit my point exactly. And almost simultaneously. All I'm trying to say is why not raise other countries up instead of bringing us down?
April 7 at 11:35am · Like · 👍 1

Figure 10.14   Praise puts you on the same side.

In the right/left game, people expect anger and epithets.

Anything outside of this realm shows respect for people. Even people you disagree with. This is part of holding the moral high ground.

If you show respect, you can ask for respect in return. If you show respect, and someone doesn't give it to you, you have every right to ask for it.

If people still don't give it to you, they look like a-holes (and yes, "a-holes" is the technical term).

Let them. Everyone else watching will side with you (remember, you're having a discussion in a public forum).

Responding to the framing of the problem, Rabbit laid out several options (Figure 10.15).

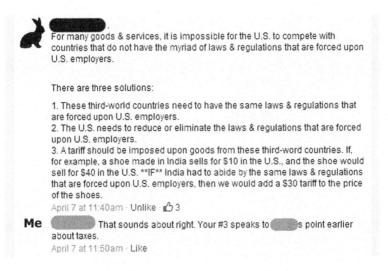

For many goods & services, it is impossible for the U.S. to compete with countries that do not have the myriad of laws & regulations that are forced upon U.S. employers.

There are three solutions:

1. These third-world countries need to have the same laws & regulations that are forced upon U.S. employers.
2. The U.S. needs to reduce or eliminate the laws & regulations that are forced upon U.S. employers.
3. A tariff should be imposed upon goods from these third-word countries. If, for example, a shoe made in India sells for $10 in the U.S., and the shoe would sell for $40 in the U.S. **IF** India had to abide by the same laws & regulations that are forced upon U.S. employers, then we would add a $30 tariff to the price of the shoes.
April 7 at 11:40am · Unlike · 👍 3

Me That sounds about right. Your #3 speaks to s point earlier about taxes.
April 7 at 11:50am · Like

Figure 10.15   Rabbit lays out the options.

I'd gotten much farther than I'd hoped. A discussion about options typically means you've agreed on the problem. Only after you've agreed on a

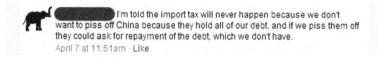

I'm told the import tax will never happen because we don't want to piss off China because they hold all of our debt, and if we piss them off they could ask for repayment of the debt, which we don't have.
April 7 at 11:51am · Like

Figure 10.16   Elephant tries to eliminate an option.

problem should you start to look at solutions. Often people try to start with solutions.

What amazed me here was I didn't even have to put together options. Rabbit did a great job and she's going to have more influence with her friends than I ever will with people who I don't even know.

Her comment even got three likes. Now my guess was that next she would try to eliminate all of the solutions she didn't like but I held back and didn't try to beat her to the punch. It was her original post and all of her friends, so I just "liked" her options and waited for the next move.

Elephant hopped on and tried to eliminate an import tax (Figure 10.16).

Then something interesting happened. A new person, Deer, jumped into the conversation (Figure 10.17).

Deer didn't seem to like all of this talk about options and came back with his belief in the market and market forces.

This was interesting because suddenly Rabbit, my friend, was being questioned by one of the more religious members of the group.

I respectfully disagree. If a country wishes to sell at below market costs, consumers should take advantage of that until market forces ultimately cause that imbalance to correct itself. Outside interference of any kind distorts a free market
April 7 at 12:39pm · Edited · Like

Figure 10.17   Rabbit is questioned by a more "religious" member.

Rabbit came back strong and said she was just pointing out options (Figure 10.18). Then she shifted the discussion back to a more recent view I've heard (mostly from David Stockman, former Reagan economic advisor) that government entitlement programs are what's keeping the market from working its magic.

I held off on commenting again for a bit. A couple of others chimed in. At this point, believe it or not, most of the work was done.

I wasn't necessarily espousing a particular solution. Just pointing out the options.

Due to overseas competition, market forces will elevate wages in India (for example) and decrease wages here in the U.S. (At least over the short term.) As the wage for a particular job decreases here in the U.S., less and less people are willing to do the job. In many cases, the wage for the job goes down to $0 in the U.S., in which case you won't find anyone to do the job.

Economists tell us this is a good thing in the long run. But they're assuming we have an idealized economic system here in the U.S., where shortages & surpluses of labor cannot occur due to supply and demand forces (i.e. if a field is high paying, people will get educated in that field and apply for those jobs, and vice-versa). The problem is that, for a large percentage of people in the U.S., there's not much incentive to get an education and work in a high-demand field (or any field for that matter). Why should someone get educated in a high-demand field when they can get on welfare or disability and make the equivalent of $12/hour for doing nothing? Our entitlement programs have put a huge monkey wrench in the supply and demand system. This is why many U.S.-based manufacturers have had a very difficult time finding workers, and why many high-tech sectors have found it necessary to import talent from overseas.

April 7 at 1:42pm · Edited · Like · 👍 2

Figure 10.18   Rabbit on the defensive.

I sat back and watched. What I wanted to do next was simply refocus the conversation if it went too far adrift and/or restate my beliefs and support with examples or facts.

Fish threw in another example of what he sees as welfare abuse: someone who wants to be on welfare after a divorce. Deer made a surprisingly good argument for Social Security (with the caveat "for those who actually paid"), and Turtle agreed with Rabbit's three recommendations. He only added a slight comment on regulations (Figure 10.19).

It's fascinating to see people apply judgment to people that they don't know. Especially people who they see as different from them. This is one reason why I believe it's so important to talk to people who are different from you. If you can see each other as both human, rather than black vs. white, or gay vs. straight, or religious vs. non-religious, it's much easier to hold conversations where you're working towards common goals.

Rabbit did a good job answering Deer and telling him that he wasn't a moocher because he had paid, but that she knew many people on disability who weren't disabled (Figure 10.20).

This is an interesting example of "good" and "bad" people. Disability insurance being OK for the "good" people but not for some evil unknowns outside the group.

10.7   Refocus where necessary

Rabbit brought up lazy people again being the problem with markets. So I simply stated what everyone already knows. Hiring in other countries is happening primarily because of low wages (Figure 10.20). Not lazy people.

Notice how once you've invoked a strong frame, your answers start to get shorter and more powerful. This is another power of evoking conceptual frames, you don't have to explain nearly as much. It may take some more work upfront to establish the strong frame, but you reap huge benefits down the road.

I refocused on the issue (lower wage workers in other countries) instead of the corporate distraction (lazy people).

Rabbit then also responded back to me that it's not just wages that fit into total cost. It's also benefits and health care and childcare and all of these freedoms people enjoy that figure into the picture.

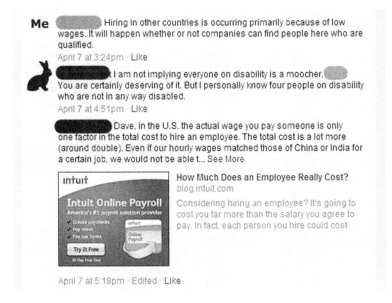

Me ⬛ Hiring in other countries is occurring primarily because of low wages. It will happen whether or not companies can find people here who are qualified.
April 7 at 3:24pm · Like

⬛ I am not implying everyone on disability is a moocher. ⬛ You are certainly deserving of it. But I personally know four people on disability who are not in any way disabled.
April 7 at 4:51pm · Like

⬛ Dave, in the U.S. the actual wage you pay someone is only one factor in the total cost to hire an employee. The total cost is a lot more (around double). Even if our hourly wages matched those of China or India for a certain job, we would not be able t... See More

intuit

Intuit Online Payroll
America's #1 payroll solution provider
✓ Create paychecks
✓ Pay taxes
✓ File tax forms
Online Payroll
Try It Free

How Much Does an Employee Really Cost?
blog.intuit.com

Considering hiring an employee? It's going to cost you far more than the salary you agree to pay. In fact, each person you hire could cost

April 7 at 5:18pm · Edited · Like

Figure 10.20   Refocus on the issue at hand.

Basically though, Rabbit and others were now trying to say that we need to reduce benefits to compete with other countries. I addressed this concern with the "equal regulations" frame earlier.

10.8   Reframe again as appropriate

Because I'd already introduced the frame of equal regulations, I just had to refer back to it.

Do we want a race to the bottom or do we want other countries to be more like ours?

I'm still holding onto the moral high ground, fighting for other countries to be more like ours. To fight for our country to be more like China or India in terms of regulations is a difficult moral fight.

I also decided I wanted to push a little further as well. I decided to push on the frame that markets are somehow natural and that we need to let them rule us.

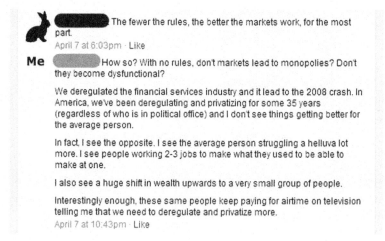

Me ⬤ It's "just right" if we want our country to be like India or China.

Markets are things we create. No?

If you don't believe me, think about how we once moved from a barter system to a system involving money. Markets didn't appear in nature before we created them.

We have the ability to make markets function any way we want (especially if they're not working particularly well). Not saying it would be easy but we write the rules for markets.
April 7 at 5:59pm · Like

Figure 10.21   Markets are things we create.

🐇 ⬤ The fewer the rules, the better the markets work, for the most part.
April 7 at 6:03pm · Like

Me ⬤ How so? With no rules, don't markets lead to monopolies? Don't they become dysfunctional?

We deregulated the financial services industry and it lead to the 2008 crash. In America, we've been deregulating and privatizing for some 35 years (regardless of who is in political office) and I don't see things getting better for the average person.

In fact, I see the opposite. I see the average person struggling a helluva lot more. I see people working 2-3 jobs to make what they used to be able to make at one.

I also see a huge shift in wealth upwards to a very small group of people.

Interestingly enough, these same people keep paying for airtime on television telling me that we need to deregulate and privatize more.
April 7 at 10:43pm · Like

Figure 10.22   In a working economy, rules are needed to ensure markets work.

So I simply pointed out how we created markets and as one of our creations, we have the ability to write the rules for markets any way we want, especially if they're not working (Figure 10.21).

The market as "force of nature" has been established so well by corporate lobbying groups that we often don't even think of challenging it. When you challenge it, however, it opens up all kinds of possibilities.

Rabbit didn't like this and came back with her belief in "less government." But she wasn't sounding so confident.

Because we were still talking and had an audience, I pushed even farther by pointing out some examples of markets breaking down and not working well in the absence of regulation (Figure 10.22).

For the record, the maxim that "The fewer the rules, the better the markets work" is a subject of debate within economics that is often mistaken for fact. While it's generally understood that perfectly competitive markets are an impossibility (like a world without friction), the belief exists that trying to get as close as possible to a perfectly competitive market is a good thing. This is a view disputed by economists.

As a quick aside, Lipsey and Lancaster have a great paper on the subject that introduced *The General Theory of the Second Best* [Lip56].

The General Theory of the Second Best states:

> If there is introduced into a general equilibrium system a constraint which prevents the attainment of one of the Paretian conditions, the other Paretian conditions, although still attainable, are, in general, no longer desirable.

In layman's terms this means that if you can't have a completely frictionless world, even trying to get as close as possible to this situation may do more harm than good.

I bring this up to illustrate that this belief in "perfect markets" is just that, a belief. You won't find supply-side economics in textbooks either. That is, there is no school of supply-side economics. Supply-side economics is a belief that was largely created by two people, Arthur Laffer, an economist of little renown, and Jude Wanniski, a journalist for the *Wall Street Journal* [Kru94].

I even added a comment about how all the pundits on TV keep trying to tell us to deregulate and privatize more.

And that was it. People stopped responding.

When this happens, I stop as well or sometimes I'll thank everyone for a good discussion. In this case, having far exceeded all of my goals as the lone liberal in a group of nine Libertarians/far-right conservatives, I stopped.

10.9 Takeaways

I have learned to enjoy talking with Tea Party members as we share a similar anger that something is deeply and fundamentally wrong with our country. To my liberal friends, this typically comes as a surprise. I show this example as a step in demonstrating that if you can get past the corporate frames and divide-and-conquer games, we're not as different as we often seem.

If you don't feel quite comfortable yet with framing, don't worry, it takes practice. Start talking about your values with people who you feel more comfortable with. If it helps, start by thinking about what you'd say to fill in the blank "I believe _____."

You'll get there.

A few things I'll highlight:

1. Speak about values. If it helps, metaphorically think of yourself as an evangelist rather than as an someone trying to win an argument or an activist trying to speak truth to power.

2. Your goal is to win people over and see if you can help them see things a little differently. Win the person, not the argument. If Satan himself had hopped on the thread, I'd be like "Honey ... holy shit ... look who just commented. Let me see if I can win him over!"

3. To do this, you have to like the person. This does *not* mean:

   (a) You have to agree with the person.

   (b) You have to be nice.

   (c) You have to be fake.

   The way I typically do this is that I find something I like about the person. For example, I've known Rabbit since college. We like similar music and have a similar sense of humor. If things ever get too serious, I try to remember these things about her and I'll put our friendship above trying to win any argument.

   In this case, I found myself liking Fish because I liked his attention to detail in the bread shop. I liked that he rotated the bread and made sure it was stocked. I imagined an older gentleman at a bread shop trying to teach his employees the rules of the bread business.

   Do I agree with his values? I agree with his work ethic. That's about it. After you find something you like about someone, though, you tend to speak to that person as if you like him. Even when you disagree. This makes all the difference in the world.

4. Hold the moral high ground. Both in terms of your values/beliefs and your behavior. In this discussion, the moral high ground to me was about the economy. I believe markets are things we create and that

we have the ability to change the rules so that they work however we desire them to work.

I also, however, held the moral high ground by never accusing anyone of being in the Tea Party, or being stupid, or even not getting it. I simply stated my beliefs, stood firm for them, respected others, and let people make up their own minds.

5. You don't have to be an economist to talk about the economy. It does, however, help to know a little bit about economics because people may try to claim an area of expertise as their domain. The field of economics these days largely undermines corporate special interest arguments. If you're looking for a place to start, a few books by economists that are quite understandable and may help with the subject are: Joseph Heath's *Economics without Illusions,* Robert Shiller's *Irrational Exuberance,* Joseph Stiglitz's *The Price of Inequality,* and Ha-Joon Chang's *23 Things They Don't Tell You About Capitalism.*

6. Understand that change occurs over the course of months and years rather than in any single discussion. It is highly unlikely that someone is going to suddenly exclaim "Eureka, I've got it!" Especially if that person holds significantly different viewpoints than you to begin with. This is why I recommend focusing most of your attention on people with more similar viewpoints.

Remember, with some people, you may be introducing new cognitive frames. This is why it's extremely important to keep your goals realistic.

With people diametrically opposed to you who've been told over and over that you are evil, your goal might just be to show them someone who isn't evil.

With someone more moderate, you might be able to go further. You might be able to build on some known conceptual frames and demonstrate how these frames apply to a new situation, such as economics.

Don't worry if it seems a bit overwhelming or unnatural at first. It takes time and practice.

PRACTICE

10.1 Find a political discussion online. Identify the frames being used in the conversation.

10.2 Find someone who believes in ''free markets." See if you can convince this person that markets are things that we create.

10.3 If you are able to convince the person in #2 that markets are things we created, state your belief in a **working economy**. Spend some time talking about how it isn't working now and how you would like to see it work for more people. If you can agree on the working market frame, see if this helps when you propose a solution.

10.4 Share what worked and any struggles with a friend or blog about it online at *Daily Kos* or another political forum.

CHAPTER 11

INFLUENCING WITHOUT AUTHORITY

> I passionately believe that's it's not just what you say that counts, it's also how you say it—that the success of your argument critically depends on your manner of presenting it.
>
> —Alain de Botton. [Law04]

Alain de Botton isn't saying anything you don't already know.

According to studies conducted by Dr. Albert Mehrabian in *Silent Messages*, 93% of communication is context, the way you look and sound, while only 7% is the words you use [Meh71].

Yet again, how often do you see people focusing exclusively on the 7%?

Here's a quick example of four ways to ask a customer service representative to transfer you with the emphasis highlighted in bold:

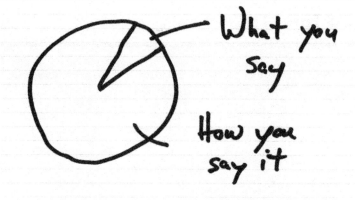

Figure 11.1   Only 7% of communication is what you say.

1. **Can** you please transfer me?

2. Can you **please** transfer me?

3. Can you please **transfer me**?

4. Can you please transfer me? (no emphasis)

"**Can** you please transfer me?" is a question within a question. Is the person able or not able to transfer you? Often, people will attest to the fact that they can transfer you and subsequently are willing to transfer you.

"Can you **please** transfer me?" sounds impatient. It would be easy for the person listening to take offense. The representative may hear it as an angry command and may not respond positively.

"Can you please **transfer me**?" can sound like an imperative, a short-tempered response, or a simple request depending on voice intonation. The first two are likely to face pushback and the last is more likely to be put through.

It is possible to say a sentence with equal emphasis: **Can you please transfer me?** Spoken in this manner, the request will usually be met with politeness in the same manner it was received.

The point is that even with simple requests, context matters much more than content.

11.1   What does "influencing without authority" mean?

The title of this chapter is borrowed from a book titled *Influence Without Authority* [Coh90]. It refers to a situation within a business environment where individuals often have to work with others who they have no authority over. In such a situation, people don't have to help you if they don't want to and building trust is key to any type of collaboration.

We face a similar situation in politics. People don't have to agree with you or work with you on anything if they don't want to. You can have all the facts and figures and arguments in the world, but someone can, for any reason whatsoever choose whether or not to agree with you.

Most people I know like this less than they would like to admit.

Coming from an academic background, I personally have struggled with this concept as in academia, there is a sense of authority even if that authority is not a person but a process. The authority process is rational and logical and opinions are subject to peer review. At least, this is the Enlightenment narrative—he who has the most logical argument wins.

If we're honest with ourselves though, even in academia we're often prone to rationalizations. How many times are decisions based on relationships? Favoritism? Animosity? Jealousy? We're very good, however, at rationalizing our own rationalizations. Still, much good comes from having standards, an approach (the scientific method), and a peer review process.

In political discussions, however, none of this exists and we often forget our situation in the heat of trying to explain some perceived "truth."

Everyone is equal and has the same right to vote. This is a characteristic of democracy.

As previously discussed, talking about values and holding the moral high ground will help you significantly when it comes to winning people over. Especially since our values are much stronger than corporate values.

In this chapter, we're going to look at a few other practices that acknowledge equality in political conversations (or lack of authority) and can help you win people over.

Before proceeding, however, I'd like to quickly revisit a subject that came up when talking about framing versus spin. Cohen and Bradford mention this as well in their preface [Coh90]:

As we have tested the ideas you are about to encounter, we discovered that plain talk about influence makes some people very uncomfortable. Explicit descriptions of how the process of influence actually works, accompanied by our advice on how to use the process, raises the spectre of manipulation to those who fear that our insights will be abused.

I've often found this to be the case as well. Many people when they hear the word "influence" think of manipulation or deceit.

A friend of mine phrased this concern as: "I believe people should make up their own minds."

Absolutely. I believe people should make up their own minds too.

When one group is fighting for *freedom* and another group is fighting for a $3 increase to the minimum wage, I can see why people would *choose* freedom. Not that an increase in the minimum wage is a bad idea, freedom is simply a much more powerful conceptual idea. When you simply talk about increasing the minimum wage, it's not clear what values you believe in.

I believe in freedom too. It's just a very different freedom than consumer choice. What I believe is that if we want to build a movement, if we want people to get involved and fight, we need to stand for something. What we, the people, should be fighting for is freedom and framing any policy issues within the context of freedom.

We should be fighting for democracy, we should be fighting for a working economy. We should be fighting for a country of people where people care about each other.

Better conceptual frames.

I want to also emphasize here that your end goal is trust and you should never say or do something you don't believe to pursue an ulterior motive. You will not be authentic and it will come back to haunt you. You want people to trust you and you want to be able to trust them. The way to do this is to be honest about your beliefs.

It's the same when you talk about values—authenticity is the difference between framing and spin. Framing is an honest expression of your beliefs, spin uses language to achieve a hidden agenda.

When conservatives say that liberals have a "hidden agenda," what they mean is that they're really fighting for something different. Talking about the minimum wage, for example, the hidden agenda is a more equitable

Figure 11.2 Bricks of character. [Ess10]

country and people who are freer because they have more time to pursue what they want out of life.

In other words, there are values behind these policies. By framing the issue, you simply acknowledge those values. In my experience, I've found people think I'm much more honest when I put my values on the table.

If people disagree with these values, great. Let's talk about it. I'll take my chances with my beliefs any day.

For example, it's easy to frame voting rights within the context of democracy when you believe in democracy. If you want to increase short-term corporate profits through a tax cut and call it "freedom" because corporate tax cuts are hard to sell, that's spin.

11.2   How do we judge character?

Typically, we focus on how the other person appears to us. We tend to be very good judges of character in others yet we may not understand how we appear to others and even if we're aware we could do better, we often don't know what to do about it. Or worse still, we dismiss the fact that people focus on 93% context and focus primarily on the 7% content.

Have you ever tried to show someone the "truth" only to be utterly and completely surprised when this person doesn't buy your beautifully constructed, fact-driven argument?

This section is a quick primer on developing skills to help possess credibility in the eyes of others. It is critical that this be accomplished through authenticity and rapport rather than intimidation or authority.

If you've known someone for a long time, you probably have a pretty good sense of this person's character. How do you assess character in someone you don't know?

Here is a sample from a cover letter written to J.P. Morgan [Che12]:

> I am unequivocally the most unflaggingly hard worker I know, and I love self-improvement. I have always felt that my time should be spent wisely, so I continuously challenge myself; I left Villanova because the work was too easy. Once I realized I could achieve a perfect GPA while holding a part-time job at NYU, I decided to redouble my effort by placing out of two classes, taking two honors classes, and holding two part-time jobs. That semester I achieved a 3.93, and in the same time I managed to bench double my bodyweight and do 35 pull-ups.

What do you think of this person? Were you impressed by the fact that he told you he could bench double his body weight and do 35 pull-ups or were you wondering why the hell he was mentioning this in a cover letter?

While I'm sure this individual is as smart as he tells us, wouldn't you be more impressed if you saw some of his work? Wouldn't this pull more weight (pun intended) than him telling you that he dropped out of Villanova because it was too easy?

You don't have to be talking about yourself either to characterize yourself. You characterize yourself by talking about other people or other things or just about anything for that matter. Depending on what you say and how you say it, people will see you as funny, as honest, as trustworthy, as conceited, as full of yourself, or negative.

Here's a quote from TV pundit Martin Bashir:

> One of the most comprehensive first-person accounts of slavery comes from the personal diary of a man called Thomas Thistlewood, who kept copious notes for 39 years....In 1756, he records that "a slave named Darby catched eating canes; had him well flogged and pickled, then made Hector, another slave, s-h-i-t in his mouth." This became known as "Darby's Dose," a punishment invented by Thistlewood that spoke only of the slave owners' savagery and inhumanity....When Mrs. Palin

invoked slavery, she doesn't just prove her rank ignorance. She confirms that if anyone truly qualified for a dose of discipline from Thomas Thistlewood, then she would be the outstanding candidate.

He is either a) willing to say anything to be controversial, b) consumed with some kind of personal beef with Palin, or c) simply a jackass. It takes a lot to make Sarah Palin look sympathetic but somehow Martin Bashir managed to do it. Does this win anyone over who didn't already hate Sarah Palin?

> Every time you characterize something or someone else, you characterize yourself.

To MSNBCs credit, they fired Bashir.

Actors have always accepted characterization. Audiences need to understand the characters in order to follow the story, and they need to grasp the essence of the characters quickly. How do actors convey character?

It may seem counter-intuitive, but they do it by the way their character characterizes everyone and everything else.

For example, Julie and Caitlin try a new restaurant famous for its fried chicken.

Caitlin says: "Their fried chicken is out of this world. It reminds me of high school and sneaking out to the Chicken Shack where they had the juiciest, spiciest fried chicken around."

Julie says: "The wait wasn't worth it. We had to stand in line for nearly 20 minutes and I can't believe the sides cost extra. They also don't give you enough napkins. I prefer a good steak anyways."

In many ways, we learn more about Julie and Caitlin by the way they relate to their experience than we do about the restaurant and the fried chicken. Through their characterization of their restaurant experience, they have also characterized themselves.

Here's Forrest Gump describing Vietnam:

> **Jenny Curran:** Were you scared in Vietnam?
> **Forrest Gump:** Yes. Well, I-I don't know. Sometimes it would stop raining long enough for the stars to come out... and then it was nice. It was like just before the sun goes to bed down on the bayou. There was always a million sparkles on the water... like that mountain lake. It was so clear, Jenny, it looked like there were two skies one on top of

Figure 11.3   George W. Bush waves from Air Force One. [Wri02]

the other. And then in the desert, when the sun comes up, I couldn't tell where heaven stopped and the earth began. It's so beautiful.

We learn from Forrest's characterizations throughout the movie more about Forrest than we do about the Vietnam War.

And yes, the movie's cheesy. And yes, it's message that optimism is the cure for everything is a vast oversimplification. We're not critiquing the movie though, we're talking about character and how what we say characterizes us.

How do we often characterize people we don't like?

What does this have the potential to say about us?

It's important to remember that when it comes to politics, what we're really typically opposed to are the ideas and the values.

For example, with George W. Bush, what I was really opposed to were the two wars and tax cuts that primarily benefitted the wealthy. In discussions with people you know who may have identified with President Bush, attacking the person may be seen as an attack on them.

If you can keep the discussion focused on the issue or value rather than the person, you increase your odds of winning people over. This also, of course, helps when the person leaves office but the ideas still remain.

Changing the ideas is much more powerful.

If a Republican or a Democrat puts in place a better economic policy, one that works for more people, do I care? What I really care about is a working economy.

11.3 The right/left game revisited

Everyone is familiar with the right/left game. It's a series of escalations where one side calls the other some form of "liberal" and the other claims the opposition is some form of "stupid" and eventually someone is compared to Hitler.

What are your odds of winning someone over if you are head to head fighting? And what does this say about you?

B-b-b-but the other side does it ... you say. They started it.

Fair enough. What's their goal? When someone tries to start this game with you by liberal baiting, what is their goal? Isn't their goal disruption? Isn't the goal divide and conquer? Do you win anything through divide and conquer?

Or, are you reading someone in the media? Remember, the goal of corporate media is to generate audience by stirring up controversy. Does your goal differ from the media?

If divide and conquer is the strategy of corporate lobbyists, wouldn't a better strategy be bringing people together and cooperating?

Have you ever won anyone over by calling them stupid?

11.4 Metaphoric relationships

Fortunately, there's a better way. Interestingly enough, it involves metaphors as well. I first encountered this practice in a leadership training [Dal12]. Here, I've adapted it to political discussions because I found there were many similarities.

To begin, I'm going to start with a couple of rules of thumb. To win someone over, you have to:

Figure 11.4   Consider metaphoric relationships.

1. Like the person.

2. Be genuine (to yourself and to the other person).

The conflict between these rules is often at the core of issues you'll have trying to win someone over.

In all likelihood, you're thinking of someone very specific right now and wondering how you're going to like that person and be sincere about it at the same time. Don't worry. We'll get there. Keep this person in mind.

My personal challenge is a guy in Florida I'll call Phil who used to work for Army Intelligence and spends every waking moment of his free time trolling liberals.

When you think about people, you tend to use metaphors. You characterize different people in your life by different roles or by what they mean to you.

A person who is a boss may also be a friend who also could be a confidant. Your wife may also be your lover who also could be an inspiration. Obviously, not all of these metaphors will be as positive. Your boss could be a roadblock or a hindrance or a royal pain in the ass.

Think of a relationship that you value for a second. One that you find rewarding and that you enjoy and see if you can identify the primary metaphoric relationship.

It may help to fill in the phrase: "You are my _____."

Some examples could be:

- Mentor

- Lover

- Accomplice

- Inspiration

- Co-conspirator

- Teacher

- Best friend

- Inspiration

- Confidante

I remember reading an article once about a boy who was saved from a shark by an uncle who dove into the water and wrestled the shark [Har01]. Thinking about my family, I wondered which of my uncles would be most likely to wrestle a shark to save someone.

Far and away, one uncle stood out. I have uncle who describes himself as "an old Florida redneck." He values family more than anything and he wouldn't hesitate for a second to punch a shark if someone's life was in danger. Uncle Steve is my "shark wrestler."

11.5 Heroes and villains

Now think of someone who you struggle with. Someone who you don't have such a positive relationship with. Someone who you find to be a difficult person.

Does this person think he or she is difficult? Does anyone wake up in the morning and say to themselves, "I'm going to really f*ck up the world today?"

Figure 11.5   I'm going to really f*ck up the world today.

Now the person may be a Mr. Burns-type character from *The Simpsons* who actually does have these thoughts. But more than likely this isn't the case.

More than likely this person believes that he or she is doing good.

We tend to self-characterize from our point of pride. This means that everyone has something that they believe they're good at and this is how they tend to see themselves.

Think back to the valuable relationship you were thinking of earlier. How would you self-characterize yourself to this person?

I am your _____.

Do you think anyone ever self-characterizes themselves as a villain?

11.6   When talent and point of pride intersect

Have you ever played the "super powers" game? That is, have you ever asked someone, if you could have one super power, what would it be?

Figure 11.6   We self-characterize from our point of pride. [Luc13]

Inherent in this game is a belief that everyone has at least one superpower. Similarly, I believe everyone has at least one talent.

When dealing with someone who, for whatever reason, I don't immediately like, I set aside my impression and I try to find this person's super power. What is this person good at?

If you pay attention, odds are good that this person will actually tell you this information, sometimes literally by saying, "I'm good at _____." or "I like to do _____."

What may look to you like "nit-picking" to them might be "attention to detail." You might think of a person as a "naysayer" while this person may think of themselves as "protecting you from bad decision" or "potential problem spotter."

Often what someone is good at relates to how they self-characterize themselves. For example, I've worked with a lot of very talented graphic designers.

One, in particular, I struggled with. I thought something looked great but this designer was never happy. I wanted to move on and this person wanted to keep working. This person was very detail-oriented and exacting when it came to something that he designed. He wanted it to have impact and he wanted the audience to immediately grasp the impact.

My goal was often quite different. I was often in a hurry and ready to get something out by deadline.

Initially, we didn't hit it off because I saw his perfectionism holding back the project and tried to convey my needs.

The result was that he didn't like working with me and would put me off making me even angrier.

I was fortunate though. A mutual friend helped me understand this person's super power as a graphic artist. He loved communicating through visuals and wanted every graphic he made to say something. If it didn't, he would work on it until it did.

So how did things change?

I started thinking of this person differently. I started thinking about this person as having this unique talent of communicating through visuals.

And when I saw a visual he made that expressed something perfectly, I told him. I didn't lie for the sake of trying to get him to like me. I just said something honest. Our relationship didn't change immediately, but eventually it changed. By recognizing what he was trying to do and his unique talent, I found I was able to give him feedback that we needed something in a hurry without making it about me and my needs.

I was able to recognize his talent and point of pride and because I recognized it and gave him credit, he was much more willing to work with me.

I never lied to him or tried to falsely flatter him. I just understood him in a way I didn't before and was able to turn him into a hero in my mind, instead of the villain he'd been before.

By looking for something to like about him, by looking for a talent, I managed to find his point of pride.

Once I saw it, I could be honest with him. I will never have his creative ability to communicate through visuals; he can make something jump off the page in a way that's instantly recognizable. In fact, he told me once that if you don't see the point of a graphic right away, the visual isn't effective.

What I did that transformed the relationship was to simply acknowledge his point of pride, his superpower. I changed nothing about him.

When you can see what a person sees in themselves and acknowledge it honestly, you have the basis for a relationship. The relationship doesn't have to be "friend." In this case, it was "visual communicator." But in

Figure 11.7 Look for the intersection of talent and point of pride. [Viz11]

many instances, it can lead in this direction. At the very least, it establishes a relationship from which you can branch out in other directions.

Over a beer at my Uncle Steve's, the shark wrestler, I brought up the story of the boy whose uncle rescued him from a shark. It was a bit risky (the beer probably helped), but I told him that we took a family vote on which uncle would most likely rescue us from a shark and that he'd won. I don't think I've ever seen anyone's face light up more. We'd hit his point of pride: he would do anything for family. When you acknowledge a talent and this talent is someone's point of pride, you usually know it.

11.7 How does this relate to political discussions?

Remember the goal: win people over.

You're not a media pundit like Bill Maher or Bill O'Reilly. You're not trying to generate controversy to increase ratings. Most often, you won't be playing to an audience.

If you want to win someone over, your chances increase dramatically if you can develop an honest relationship with this person. Finding a positive metaphor helps.

Phil is my biggest personal challenge. When I first met Phil, online, I couldn't stand him. I thought he was arrogant, full of himself, conceited, and wrong on every topic under the sun.

We had epic comment battles that raged for pages over the course of weeks. Mostly, because it drove me crazy how he could hold certain opinions.

Shortly after I learned about this idea of metaphoric relationships, I decided to try to think a little differently about Phil. What was his talent?

Off the top of my head, here's what I came up with:

- **Quoter of '80s movies:** He loves to quote from movies. Particularly, '80s movies of the Sly Stallone/Die Hard kind.

- **Home security expert:** He is ex-military and owns his own business where he sells security equipment.

- **Instigator:** There is no one I know who can liberal bait like Phil. He knows every trick in the book. He seems to hate liberals and has made it his mission to figure out how to get under their skin. His favorite trick is to accuse liberals of what conservatives are doing. So he'll accuse liberals of racism, of class warfare, of elitism. You name it.

- **Last-word-getter:** One of the other things about Phil that drives most people nuts is that somewhere down the road, someone must have taught him that whoever gets in the last word wins. He will always get in the last word. I've tested his resolve and he won. No matter how ridiculous it gets, he will get in the last word.

Because his instigation skills are part of what drives me nuts, I decided that I couldn't honestly compliment him in this area. '80s movie quotes were an easy one but this isn't what I would call his core point of pride. His core point of pride is as an ex-military officer. However, one of the biggest things we've fought over through the years has been our country's security policies. So I wasn't about to cede this area of expertise to him.

But home security. This was an area I knew little about and actually had a bit of an interest in. I wanted to know if there was a home security system that could be purchased once and didn't have monthly fees.

So during the course of one of our discussions, I asked him if I could contact him offline about security systems. I made sure to stay out of politics during the discussion and kept the topic on home security systems. He told me about a couple options and actually seemed to be flattered that I asked. I thanked him sincerely (because this was great information!) and then we went back to our normal banter.

Did I win him over?

No and yes. Phil will bait liberals from his deathbed. However, I did win him over enough that we often talk about other things and he was willing to help me out. He's also asked me for advice on computers and installing a Nest home thermostat. So I was able to reciprocate.

After this, I found that our political conversations tended to show more respect for the other person. Whenever things started to get a little heated, I'd make a joke and soon, I found, he started to do it too.

In other words, we came to an understanding. Sometimes, that's all you can ask for. The beautiful thing is, that after I realized I would never win Phil over, I discovered something else valuable about Phil.

He knows conservative arguments so well and has fought for so long that I found I could test out entire positions and frames with him. If there was a hole, he'd find it. If there wasn't, he'd attack as best he could or try to change the subject.

He was like playing against a wall in a game of tennis. You would never beat the wall, but if you practiced against the wall, it made you better.

I need only one hand to count the number of times I've won Phil over to a point of view. And I have at least three fingers to spare. But I've won over countless other people because I've fleshed out my values and opinions with Phil beforehand.

He is my home security consultant and political tennis wall. Someday, I hope to meet him in person.

11.8 Ground rules

The secret to transforming the way we relate to people with different value frames is to ask:

- What is their internal truth?
- How do they see themselves?

Here are a few steps:

- Identify your metaphoric relationship: "You are my _____." (In many cases, this may start out as political enemy/opponent.)

- Recognize a talent.

- Give up the need to be right.

- Discover how they view themselves: "I am your _____."

- Create a new metaphoric relationship.

- Build on the relationship. Only after you've established a relationship should you have any real political conversations.

Note: No lying!

You must acknowledge their point of pride truthfully even if it is only a small part of the thing that is the most important thing in the world to them. Otherwise, it will not be authentic and they will know you are not authentic. Find the talent to like or admire and acknowledge it truthfully and publicly.

This builds credibility and mutual respect.

Not only that, but if you can find something to like about someone, you'll be surprised how your approach changes. You talk differently. Your expressions change. You act more like yourself. Think about when you're talking with friends. You literally feel different, express yourself differently, and have more confidence.

When you have this type of relationship, you can talk openly about difficult subjects like politics and you are both more likely to listen and be heard.

Treating people in this manner will also help you hold the moral high ground.

PRACTICE

11.1   Think of someone close to you. What is your metaphoric relationship with this person? That is, how would you fill in the phrase: You are my _____.

11.2   Pick someone you know and find challenging. How do you think this person characterizes herself or himself? What is this person's "super power"?

11.3   Consider again the person you identified in #2. How might you establish a relationship? How might you view this person's '"super power" as valuable? Does this open up new areas for conversation?

CHAPTER 12

COMMON DENOMINATORS IN CORPORATE FRAMING

If these out-of-date beliefs are to be called myths, then myths can be produced by the same sorts of methods and held for the same sorts of reasons that now lead to scientific knowledge.

—Thomas Kuhn, 1962. [Kuh62]

George Lakoff and others have written extensively about corporate framing. Lakoff isolated the key element in corporate framing as strict father morality.

From *Don't Think of an Elephant* [Lak04]:

When children do something wrong, if they are physically disciplined they learn not to do it again. That means they will develop an internal discipline to keep themselves from doing wrong, so that in the future they will be obedient and act morally. Without such punishment, the world will go to hell. There will be no morality.

There is a corresponding link to capitalism. In capitalism, the market is viewed as the strict father, rewarding those who are good and punishing those aren't with poverty.

In this view of the world, poverty is viewed as a just reward for those who are deemed unworthy. Anyone who tries to help these people is viewed as interfering with a punishment that is deserved.

From a moral standpoint, strict father morality is against nurturance and care. You will see this reflected in language like "coddled" or "nanny state" or "adult in the room."

The progressive version of parenting, on the other hand, Lakoff calls the nurturant parent model. It is based on empathy and responsibility. I think of this as the two-parent model.

Lakoff goes into much more detail if you're interested and/or haven't seen his analysis before. I introduce it because so often what I hear is that conservatives are some version of "crazy." Again, I'd like to emphasize that they're not crazy. They're simply reasoning from strictly conservative cognitive value frames.

These frames have been honed and repurposed over the years by corporate special interests groups and have been found to be particularly effective as part of a divide-and-conquer strategy.

You know these frames: the free market, individual freedom, the traditional (father as patriarch) family, better strong and wrong than weak. You also know what conservatives think of liberals (Hint: they're weak and effeminate and foreign).

For this reason, I'm not going go into great detail about the frames themselves.

Instead, I want to look at some of the common denominators, why they're of great interest to corporate lobbying groups, and how you can connect with people who typically share both progressive *and* conservative values.

12.1   Limiting options

Have you ever wondered why more people aren't fighting back against the corporate takeover of America?

This was essentially the question behind Thomas Frank's groundbreaking book *What's the Matter with Kansas?*

Another way to put this is why do people vote against their own self-interest?

People economically alienated by corporate America should be flocking to a political party that represents their interests. The trouble according to Frank [Fra04] is that:

> Culturally speaking, however, that option is simply no longer available to them anymore. Democrats no longer speak to the people on the losing end of a free-market system that is becoming more brutal and more arrogant by the day.
>
> The problem is not that Democrats are monolithically pro-choice or anti-school prayer; it's that by dropping the class language that once distinguished them sharply from Republicans they have left themselves vulnerable to cultural wedge issues like guns and abortion and the rest whose hallucinatory appeal would ordinarily be far overshadowed by material concerns.

According to Frank, Republicans are the only party talking about class. But they talk about class in a different way, they talk about "elite liberals." They turn people against their own self-interests by finding a different elitism for them to hate, an elitism not of wealth or power but of culture.

Franks's assessment holds true to this day. Though with the economic collapse of 2008, corporate propagandists had to work overtime to find new scapegoats.

Fortunately, they had help from the conceptual frames they'd developed. These frames often limit "agency." In other words, they encourage inaction.

The frame used most often to limit agency is an economic one: "let the markets work." In this version of the story, not only is it wrong to interfere with markets, but we're told that "interfering" with markets will actually cause harm.

If you're talking to someone who believes in this concept of markets, they reason from the belief that the market is a natural thing and that a greater good always comes from letting the "market work."

Most economists will tell you differently. But remember, we're not talking about economics. We're talking about a conceptual story told by corporate special interest groups that has elements of economics and elements of religion. The veil of economics is used to hide the religion.

Economists will talk about how markets can reach an equilibrium between supply and demand and how markets can help allocate resources efficiently, but they would never go so far as to tell you this will always lead to a "greater good."

Economic thought today largely accepts that markets behave irrationally (because of the works of people like George Akerlof, Robert Shiller, and others) and that, even if markets could behave perfectly rationally, there's no guarantee that a greater good would be served.

You're likely not talking to an economist though. You're talking to people who believe in a conceptual idea that unregulated markets always serve a greater good and are always the best solution.

12.1.1   Creating space

So how do you break them out of this market fundamentalism?

Start with the basics. I've found that it helps to literally establish that people created markets. Markets are not something found in nature.

Talk about the barter system. Talk about the creation of money. Talk about the creation of limited liability corporations. Talk about the invention of credit. Talk about interest. Talk about the history behind the creation of markets.

After you establish that people created markets and that they're not some natural force, it's much easier to see that we can create these markets towards different ends.

We can create markets so they benefit many people or benefit a select few.

Instead of arguing with them, empower them with the ability to change things and then work to win them over to a more realistic view of markets.

Because make no mistake about it, many of these frames are designed to keep people from fighting back or, more typically, to channel the ways in which they fight in a desired direction. For example, it's OK to "vote with your money" but they'll tell you it's not worth voting for politicians because "all politicians are the same."

You're supposed to "let markets work," but people in power are free to lobby government for any type of handout or assistance they want.

When you think about it, the reason is obvious.

In a democracy, you have an equal vote. Everyone's vote has the same weight. In a market, if we vote only with our dollars, those with the most dollars always win.

Given this is the case, why would anyone want to give up their equal vote?

The answer is no one would or does. Not if they're thinking within the frame of democracy.

But if the wealthy can convince people that the economic system of markets makes a better political system (where a greater good is somehow naturally maximized), many people may start to reason within this frame.

Missives like this tend to be quite popular and widely circulated:

> A democracy will continue to exist up until the time that voters discover
> that they can vote themselves largesse from the public treasury.

Forget for a second that this quote is often wrongly attributed to Ben Franklin, Alexis de Tocqueville, Thomas Jefferson, or Alexander Hamilton [Col09].

Focus on the belief behind the quote. The belief is that people will vote for their own self-interests.

What's wrong with that you say? Well, nothing. Unless you are a large corporation subject to oversight from the people and you would rather not have that oversight.

Why is it OK, for example, to act selfishly in a market but not to act in your best interests when you vote?

The answer, when you think about it, is that it doesn't make any sense. Corporations spend millions each year lobbying the government for what they want and then turn around and tell you that you're not supposed to vote for your interests.

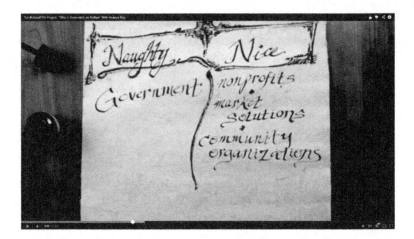

Figure 12.1   Corporate value frames often limit options in a direction that favors corporations.

A closer view of reality would be that our democracy is in danger because corporations have discovered they can purchase the political system through campaign contributions and marketing campaigns.

Ananya Roy, a professor of city and regional planning and Distinguished Chair in Global Poverty and Practice at UC Berkeley produced a wonderful video describing her experiences with her yearly class on global poverty [Roy13].

In the video, she describes how the post-welfare generation, the generation born after Reagan, has come to view government as "bad."

In Roy's words:

> They had grown up in an era in which welfare, not poverty, had become
> the problem to be solved. I realized that afternoon that this post welfare
> generation was also expressing deep ambivalence about the role of gov-
> ernment. They liked non-profits. They liked market solutions to poverty.
> They liked community organizations. But they did not like government.

Of course they didn't like government. They've been told all of their lives, to quote Reagan, that "government is not the solution to our problems, government is the problem."

In the past, when people were angry at low wages and poverty, people had different outlets. The news would report on issues, identify causes, and we, the people, could influence our legislators to solve problems. Unions formed to equalize power relationships with large employers.

Now, we're told not to act. We're told that we, the people, are the problem. We're told we can act in any way but through government. We can make purchases. We can form non-profit advocacy organizations (which typically don't have the power to take on corporations), but we can't act through government.

We've been told this because some business leaders want more power and less responsibility.

Keep in mind, I'm not saying government will always be the best solution. But why take it off the table before the discussion even begins?

This is why it's so important before talking about any kind of solution to first create the space to look at all available solutions.

Here are a few questions I ask to break down some of these frames (especially the market ones) and create space for other options:

- Who created markets?

- Why is one type of organization OK, but another not? (Why is it OK to organize as a corporation or interest group, but not as a community, state, union, or country?)

- Why are people who don't believe in government running for office? Isn't this a conflict of interest?

- Why is it OK for wealthy people to run/influence government through lobbying and money?

- What happens when markets don't work?

- What about situations where poorly regulated markets haven't worked so well (health care, cable TV, the food industry of Upton Sinclair's *The Jungle*, child labor, slavery, global sex trade)?

Roy, in her class, breaks down the conceptual walls by talking about middle class welfare. Most people in the middle class don't think of themselves as benefiting from government. Yet far and away more people in the middle and upper classes receive benefits from the government than do the poor.

In 2013, for example, the entire Department of Housing and Urban Development (HUD) had a budget of roughly $44 billion for housing assistance for the nation's poor [HUD13]. Deductions of mortgage interest, for middle-class and wealthy homeowners, were estimated to cost $70 billion in this same year, nearly twice the budget for HUD. 77% of these benefits go to people with incomes over $100,000 a year while more than half of home owners receive no benefit [Fis13].

Roy illustrates that the wealthy receive far more welfare than most people think. Brilliant.

The important thing to remember is that if you don't create this conceptual "space," people may not even be willing to talk about government solutions.

Are Roy's students stupid? Most people wouldn't say that about students attending UC Berkeley. I would argue, however, that the same thing that's going on with Roy's students is going on with many, many others across America. Unfortunately, not everyone has a Professor Roy capable of breaking down corporate framing and showing them better frames.

This is why it's so important when you're talking to people you know to first understand the conceptual frames they're using.

If you understand the frames they're reasoning from, you can start at the appropriate point in a discussion. What may seem obvious to you, may not seem obvious to them.

Just remember that many of these frames encourage inaction, especially of the government kind. You will get nowhere with any type of government solution if this is an intrinsic belief.

If you reframe government as democracy and markets as things we create within the context of a democracy, however, you significantly improve your odds of being able to talk about solutions.

12.2 "Good" people vs. "bad" people

If someone believes in strict father morality, selfishness, and individuality, how is it that they're able to help their own kids? Or their own families? Or their own friends?

Quite simply, many people are perfectly comfortable applying strict father morality to others while believing in more nurturant values when it comes to their families, friends, and acquaintances.

Corporate divide-and-conquer strategies take advantage of this idea: create a group, make that group "good," find an enemy for that group, and pit the two against each other.

A friend of mine believes that government welfare policies have destroyed the black family. He would agree with the sentiments of Cliven Bundy, the Nevada rancher who spoke out against welfare. Bundy had this to say about African-Americans and welfare [Nag13]:

> They abort their young children, they put their young men in jail because they never learned how to pick cotton. And I've often wondered, are they better off as slaves, picking cotton and having a family life and doing things, or are they better off under government subsidy? They didn't get no more freedom. They got less freedom.

What's odd (outside of the fact that Mr. Bundy seems to think slavery was good) about this statement is that Mr. Bundy is focusing only on black families. A group of people unfamiliar to him (black people) he views through the eyes of a group that he belongs to (white people). One group is "good." The other is "bad".

He doesn't even seem to consider that if this were the case, shouldn't it have also happened to poor white families? If so, this would bolster his argument against welfare.

He wants to apply strict father morality (punishment) to the "other" group while he makes no mention that the "deserving" group ever receives welfare.

This same friend made a quite different comment when a disabled friend told him that he needed disability.

> I am not implying everyone on disability is a moocher. You are certainly deserving of it.

He literally sees two classes of people. There are the "good" people, people he sees as upstanding and deserving. These people are typically people he knows and is familiar with. Then there are the "bad" or immoral people who deserve punishment.

12.2.1 Expanding the definition of "good" people

One strategy I could have employed was to call my friend a racist.

However, this would pit us against each other as enemies. This would have accomplished little. My goal is to help him learn and grow and overcome something that I have struggled for years (and will likely always struggle) to overcome.

So instead of approaching the issue as me (not racist) versus him (racist), I tried to approach the situation as me (recovering racist) and him (recovering racist).

I attempted to break down the groups he sees. Ananya Roy did this in the previous example on welfare by showing that most welfare goes to middle class people and the wealthy.

I asked my friend why white families weren't destroyed by welfare.

White and black people make up a roughly equal proportion of those on welfare (38.8% white to 39.8% black according to 2014 Department of Health and Human Services statistics). If welfare destroys families, then shouldn't it destroy white families as well?

I then switched back to Cliven Bundy and asked why he, specifically, deserves $1 million in tax breaks (taxes that he hasn't paid over the past 20 years). I painted him as the selfish moocher he is and not some heroic "freedom" fighter.

> It's just funny that when a wealthy white rancher receives over $1 mllion
> in government handouts, he's somehow a "freedom fighter." Let's just
> call this guy what he is, a deadbeat moocher welfare queen.

In other words, I held the moral high ground.

Instead of arguing, he tried to change the subject to find a different moral high ground. When this happens, you know you have the moral high ground.

Don't take the bait. I continued to break down the groups he had defined as "good" and "bad."

When you hold the moral high ground, you will know it. Hold it. Don't let it go. Continue to express your belief strongly without attacking the person.

You win by showing that people have more in common than we think rather than perpetuating group fight. When you can break down barriers between "good" and "bad," people are more likely to want to help everyone and less likely to want to punish the perceived "bad" group.

If someone continues to argue that somehow one group is inherently "good" and another is "bad," keep asking the question: "Why?" If they want to continue along these lines, let them. They will lose in the court of public opinion.

This approach also works well with the religious because this idea of "good" and "bad" people exists in many religions. The idea that wealth, for example, is a sign from God that a person is "good" in some Calvinist Christian religions, for example.

Of course this goes against the teachings of Christ [Bib78].

> **Mark 12:41-44** Jesus sat down opposite the place where the offerings were put, and watched the crowd putting their money into the temple treasury. Many rich people threw in large amounts. But poor widow came and put in two very small copper coins, worth only a fraction of a penny. Calling his disciples to him, Jesus said, "I tell you the truth, this poor widow has put more into the treasury than all the others. They all gave out of their wealth; but she, out of her poverty, put in everything— all she had to live on."

> **Luke 14:12-14** Then Jesus said to his host, "When you give a luncheon or dinner, do not invite your friends, your brothers or relatives, or your rich neighbors; if you do, they may invite you back and so you will be repaid. But when you give a banquet, invite the poor, the crippled, the lame, the blind, and you will be blessed. Although they cannot repay you, you will be repaid at the resurrection of the righteous."

> **Luke 6:20-21** Looking at his disciples, he said: "Blessed are you who are poor, for yours is the kingdom of God."

You get the picture.

I've found it's easy to speak with Christians when I respect their beliefs and simply express mine. This is because, contrary to the story told by many political pundits, Christian beliefs and the beliefs of non-Christians are typically very similar. Both typically believe in mutual responsibility, democracy, freedom, working markets, and equality.

If I hear a version of "good" people vs. "bad" people like Christians vs. non-Christians, one option is to break down these barriers.

12.3 Telling only part of the story

One of the other tricks of corporate frames is putting an extreme emphasis on part of a particular value or belief.

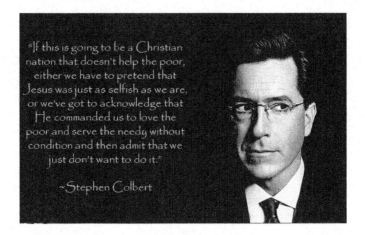

"If this is going to be a Christian nation that doesn't help the poor, either we have to pretend that Jesus was just as selfish as we are, or we've got to acknowledge that He commanded us to love the poor and serve the needy without condition and then admit that we just don't want to do it."

~Stephen Colbert

Figure 12.2   How can we be a Christian nation that doesn't care about our poor?

The easiest way to think about this is to think about Lakoff's two views of parenting: strict father parenting and nurturant parenting.

Strict father parents emphasize punishment and personal responsibility. Nurturant parents believe in teaching and educating and helping their children grow into adulthood.

Corporations have chosen to emphasize *only* values from strict father parenting because they've found it serves a purpose (for them). Most people, however, hold both views and simply choose to use them in different situations with their children.

For example, there are times when even nurturant parents find punishment appropriate. And times when strict father parents believe in encouragement.

However, since the strategy is divide and conquer, corporate frames typically pit people against each other.

You hear: "You're either with us, or against us." You hear the strict father "My way or the highway." You hear that liberals are the mommy party and conservatives are the daddy party when isn't what we really want a "mommy and daddy" party?

Corporate framing plays to extremes with the goal of dividing and conquering.

12.3.1   Expanding conceptual frames

If you can start from a point of commonality, you stand a much better chance of winning someone over. A great example to build off of is personal responsibility.

Other examples of corporate frames that are subsets of much better frames include:

Corporate framing	Reframing/Expansion
Smaller government	**Democracy** and non-corrupt government. We want a government up to the task, whatever the task may be. We need a government by and for the people with sufficient power to be able to create a working economy.
Personal responsibility	**Mutual responsibility**. Responsibility not just to oneself but also to others and the community.
Laissez-faire capitalism or free markets	**Working economy.** Appropriate rules and structure lead to an economy that works for more people and is fair for small business.
Selfishness	**Freedom** and **mutual responsibility**. True freedom involves not simply selfishness but respect and concern for others.
Capitalism	**Democracy.** Capitalism without government is a black market.

Table 12.1   Expanding on corporate frames.

I think personal responsibility is great. Most everyone I know does too. The only problem I have is when this is the only value being discussed.

In other words, I believe personal responsibility is a subset of mutual responsibility.

Mutual responsibility involves both a responsibility to yourself and also a responsibility to others and the community. Personal responsibility, on the other hand, the way it is discussed by corporate special interest groups, is completely self-focused.

Corporate interest groups preach personal responsibility because when people fight against each other, they win. They remove responsibility for others and the community from the corporate docket and put people into bidding wars against each other.

Nevertheless, when someone brings up personal responsibility, it's not a bad idea to build off this and expand the concept to mutual responsibility.

In this manner, you connect the idea to something that you both believe. It costs you nothing to talk about the importance of personal responsibility, you gain credibility by giving credit where credit is due, and then you can demonstrate how to take the idea further.

PRACTICE

12.1   Consider someone you know who believes in "good" people and "bad" people. Who is "in" the good category and who is "out"? What are some examples that might challenge these lines?

12.2   What examples or stories might you use to break people out of the limiting notion that the market always comes up with the best solution?

12.3   What stories from your personal experience expand on a limiting corporate frame? Which are most powerful?

12.4   Try telling your most powerful story to a friend. Write or share about how your story was received.

CHAPTER 13

OVERCOMING OBJECTIONS

If there is a problem you can't solve, then there is an easier problem you can solve: find it.

—George Pólya. [Kuh62]

The best strategies for overcoming objections are those that anticipate objections in the first place.

Speaking about your beliefs is such an approach. The good news is that refining your target audience and goal and simply talking about your values will help you avoid many of the most heated battles. Caring about and respecting people more than winning an argument will also help you in this respect.

Eventually, however, you will encounter situations where you'll face objections.

After people have bought into a philosophy they can be, how shall I say it, "religious" about it. When you're talking about people's beliefs, often you're talking about something that has become a core part of their identity, and when threatened, may trigger an emotional response.

There's no need to be afraid of these situations, however. Especially if you're prepared.

Here, we'll focus on a few strategies for overcoming objections.

13.1   Objections are expressions of emotional need

It's accepted knowledge among sales people that buying is an emotional decision.

Think about someone you know who recently made a purchase. The example I'm going to use is a car. Cars make a great example because people frequently buy cars that express their identity.

Figure 13.1   1964 Corvette convertible.

If people want to be seen as caring about the environment, for example, they might buy a Prius or a Chevy Volt. If they want to be seen as rebellious or free, they might buy a Corvette or a convertible. People hate minivans because minivans are a practical vehicle. Minivans express that you have kids. Enter the sports utility vehicle—you can be practical and still express yourself!

You get the picture. People buy based on emotions.

Michael Bosworth and John Holland sum up what good sales people know [Bos03]:

> When a buyer decides to buy from a particular seller, it is an emotional decision. Equally, when a buying committee decides to buy from a particular vendor, it is an emotional decision. When a buyer decides to pay an asking price rather than holding out for a lower price, it is an emotional decision. When a buyer decides to buy from a person he or she is comfortable with, rather than shopping for the lowest possible price, it is an emotional decision.

Yet when you talk to people about their car-buying decision, they often say things like:

- "I got a really good deal."
- "My old car was about to die."
- "It gets great gas mileage."
- "It will increase in value."
- "No one else makes engines like this."

In other words, they rationalize their emotional decision.

The decision itself comes down to emotions. But when people justify their decision to others, they'll use logic and reason. This is, I believe, because we idealize rational or computer-like decisions. People are expected to make "rational" decisions so we back up our emotional decisions with data or rational arguments to explain decisions to others without social risk.

The research of Westen, Lakoff, Nyhan, Reifler, and others leads us to believe that people make political decisions in a very similar fashion, based on cognitive value frames and emotion.

If we think about objections in the traditional academic sense, we may see an objection as a logical argument. If we think of objections as logical objections, our gut response is going to be to rush to overcome the objection with facts and data.

Has a sales person ever tried to sell you something before you were ready? Have you ever felt pushed by a sales person?

The same thing can happen in political conversations if you try to "tell someone" about the best solution. This is what conservatives mean when they say "liberals will try to tell you what's right." What's more convincing: when someone tries to "tell you" something or when you figure it out for yourself?

The difficulty we face is that when we've done a great deal of research on solutions and believe we know what the best solution is, it's easy to be impatient with people and want to jump to solutions. Or jump to trying to overcome an objection with the entire arsenal of facts and data at your disposal.

A colleague I used to work with gave me a piece of advice once about how to view objections. To this day I remember his advice:

> An objection is an expression of emotional need.

For me, this cut against the grain of everything I'd learned. In the academic realm, objections are typically questions raised based on research or someone's own scientific experiences. In the academic world, objections are scientific objections (at least that's the claim of science).

Politics has much more in common with sales and my experience matches my colleague's advice: objections are an expression of emotional need.

If you start with emotional need as an underlying assumption, you'll approach the situation differently.

Here's a framework for overcoming objections based on my experiences in political discussions.

1. **Listen.** The first thing you want to do is make sure you listen to the objection. Often, we're so eager to explain our own point of view that we sweep right past what the other person is saying.

2. **Acknowledge.** Acknowledge honestly the fact or need being expressed. One way to do this is to repeat what the person is saying in your own words. I will often say something like "Let me make sure I understand what you're saying " and then phrase back what they've said in my own words.

   Be honest. Avoid clichés like "I know you feel."

3. **Ask questions.** The emotional need may not be obvious from the surface objection. A great example of this is climate change. I know many people who believe in climate change but will strongly argue the

corporate line that science is divided.

Asking questions, I found out that people who are against climate change often believe that coping with climate change will kill jobs. This is an emotional fear that has little to do with the science of climate change itself. Claiming science is divided on the issue is simply the rationalization.

4. **Address their need.** This will vary by situation, but here it's critical to have an understanding of facts and solutions. Please don't think I'm claiming that facts and solutions aren't important. They're critical. I've simply found that it's much more effective if you use them at the right time; we often start too early.

After you understand the emotional need, address it.

In the case where people are afraid dealing with climate change might kill jobs, for example, it's important to lay out the economic case. Sticking with my climate change example, if the emotional need is jobs, I will talk about the economic opportunity we have for developing clean energy technologies. I'll talk about success stories like Germany and how we, in the U.S., should be leading when it comes to technology instead of following. Knowing the emotional need allows you to have a real conversation with people instead of simply calling them "climate deniers" and throwing a mountain of scientific research at them.

5. **Restate your belief.** This relates back to the five frames. You want to be sure people understand how any solution is also moral (the right thing to do). Because when it comes to politics, people make decisions at the emotional level, the level of right and wrong.

In the case of climate change, I would relate this back to my belief in a working economy. In a working economy, we should be making sure that resources that are available to us are available to our children. A working economy should be sustainable. An economy based around a finite resource like oil is not sustainable. It might help us short term, but long term we should be working to develop a sustainable economy.

Remember, when you're introducing a new conceptual frame to someone, it's going to take time at first. This is where repetition and different ways of explaining your belief—personal stories, anecdotes, examples, studies, and so on—help people to understand.

6. **Ask for feedback.** Remember it's a conversation. Though this is listed as step #6, this really should be done throughout.

   - What are your thoughts?

   - What have you experienced?

   People are more likely to believe you if you help them get there themselves. Let them propose solutions, let them ask questions, let them talk about their experiences. I've found that if I think of myself as a guide more than a political activist, I tend to have much better conversations. And quite often, I've found I've learned as much or more than I've been able to help. In any situation, you are always both guide and student.

7. **Repeat various steps as necessary.** Though I've laid this out in a numbered format, in conversations you're quite likely to go through many of these steps multiple times. Don't get frustrated. It's a process. Repeat as needed and remember that if someone is still talking with you, they're still somehow interested.

I should also mention that this process works best in a one-on-one situation where you can have a conversation and there's no fear of an audience. The same process works for groups, however, you just have to also take into account group dynamics and facilitation.

Again, be honest. You win nothing by deceit. Mean what you say and always remember to frame issues and any potential solutions within the context of your values.

13.2   What to do if someone treats you like an enemy

Let's be honest. You're going to encounter people who you're not going to be able to win over. Not in the short term or possibly ever.

The corporate world understands this and plays it up: anyone who disagrees with you is a liberal and liberals are the enemy, they are communists, they will try to tell you what to think. Stop at nothing when dealing with liberals because they will stop at nothing in dealing with you.

Then, what do we often try as our first step? We trigger the defense mechanism by getting into an argument.

Fortunately, most people aren't this extreme. If you do find yourself in one of these situations, however (and it's inevitable), tell the person that you need to agree to disagree. Or simply say that you'd rather talk about something else than risk your friendship.

We lost an uncle long ago to *Fox and Friends*. He feels the need to evangelize at every family get-together. Every occasion merits a dose of anti-government rage.

I know I won't win him over. I also know I don't want to listen to him. So I respectfully suggest that we not talk about politics. He usually tries to bait me into a discussion once or twice after my suggestion but I've found that if I don't take the bait and repeat my request, he'll stop. If he doesn't stop, he looks like an a-hole (technical term).

If someone won't respect your wishes, walk away. Focus on better objectives with people more willing to keep an open mind. This is someone incapable of respecting boundaries. You don't have to listen.

13.3   Win the audience

This strategy assumes there is an audience. Examples include group settings and online forums.

This is a particularly powerful strategy if you can pull it off but don't try this unless you have practiced with individuals, feel comfortable in a group setting, and know you can keep a cool head.

The idea is simple.

The situation looks like this: You've tried to win someone over and its become clear that this person is going to be against you no matter what.

At this point, and only at this point, you may want to shift gears and think about the audience. If you've been working on holding the moral high ground in individual conversations, the principle, when applied to an audience, is very similar: you want to be seen as the one "in the right."

Once again, however, this is very different from having "the better argument" in the traditional academic sense of the word. If what I just said still makes you feel uncomfortable, this is not a strategy for you.

If you still think this is about "messaging," this is not a strategy for you.

If, however, you feel comfortable talking about your beliefs and have also started to feel comfortable with the idea of winning people over, you may be interested in giving it a try. At the very least, you should recognize how people in the media use this tactic.

Here's an excerpt from the movie *Thank You for Smoking* [Rei05]:

> **Joey Naylor:** ... so what happens when you're wrong?
> **Nick Naylor:** Whoa, Joey I'm never wrong.
> **Joey Naylor:** But you can't always be right ...
> **Nick Naylor:** Well, if it's your job to be right, then you're never wrong.
> **Joey Naylor:** But what if you are wrong?
> **Nick Naylor:** OK, let's say that you're defending chocolate, and I'm defending vanilla. Now if I were to say to you: "Vanilla is the best flavor ice-cream," you'd say...
> **Joey Naylor:** No, chocolate is.
> **Nick Naylor:** Exactly, but you can't win that argument ... so, I'll ask you: so you think chocolate is the end all and the "be all" of ice-cream, do you?
> **Joey Naylor:** It's the best ice-cream, I wouldn't order any other.
> **Nick Naylor:** Oh! So it's all chocolate for you is it?
> **Joey Naylor:** Yes, chocolate is all I need.
> **Nick Naylor:** Well, I need more than chocolate, and for that matter I need more than vanilla. I believe that we need freedom. And choice when it comes to our ice-cream, and that Joey Naylor, that is the definition of liberty.
> **Joey Naylor:** But that's not what we're talking about
> **Nick Naylor:** Ah! But that's what I'm talking about.
> **Joey Naylor:** ... but you didn't prove that vanilla was the best ...
> **Nick Naylor:** I didn't have to. I proved that you're wrong, and if you're wrong I'm right.
> **Joey Naylor:** But you still didn't convince me.
> **Nick Naylor:** It's not you that I'm after. I'm after them.
> *(points into the crowd)*

So what do you have to do differently? Not much.

The biggest difference is that your focus is on winning over the audience as the target rather than the person you are speaking with.

If you can, stake out your moral position in advance. Understand how your opponent is most likely to try to stake out their position and know how to defend yours.

Facts are important, but facts without the ability to make a strong case for a better belief (conceptual frame) are useless.

PRACTICE

13.1   What objections do you hear the most? What is the underlying emotional need?

13.2   Have you ever gotten into a conversation and said something you regretted? What happened? How would you handle the situation differently if you could go back in time?

13.3   Has there ever been a time when you avoided a political conversation because you feared a fight of some sort?

13.4   Is it acceptable for everyone in our culture to state their beliefs? Or is it more acceptable for some than others? Why or why not?

PART V

CLOSE

CHAPTER 14

A VIRTUAL UNION

If you want to build a big movement, pick a big fight.
—Derek Cressman, 2014 [Cre14].

Lawrence Lessig asked a great question in an essay in *The Atlantic*: Why is money in politics almost never a voting issue? [Les14]

Given that 90% of Americans believe it's important to reduce the influence of money in politics according to a recent Global Strategy Group (GSG) poll, why don't people vote based on the issue?

Lessig believes people feel they simply won't get reform so they move on. The same poll from GSG said that more that 90% believe the influence won't be reduced anytime soon. So we resign ourselves to the situation and move on to other issues.

Even more cynically, according to a 2012 Clarus Research Group poll, 80% of Americans said they thought any reforms were designed to "help current members of Congress get re-elected."

In Lessig's words:

> We want reform. We just don't trust that we can actually get it. We believe we have a corrupt system. But we don't believe insiders when they tell us they will fix it.

I've had this discussion many, many times with people from across the political spectrum. People who self-identify as Republicans believe any reforms are designed to help Democrats. People who self-identify as Democrats believe reform is impossible because Republicans will never support it.

In other words, the issue has been reduced to the usual Republican/Democrat back and forth.

Reform's greatest challenge, Lessig believes, is this "politics of resignation."

Lessig calls for a moonshot movement, something to crack the cynicism, something that will engage and rally people. Something that's different from politics as usual.

I believe a moonshot is exactly what's needed.

14.1   A recent experience

Recently, I attended the Invest in Neighborhoods (IIN) conference in Cincinnati. IIN is a nonprofit organization created to help the 51 community councils and other groups that represent the Cincinnati's neighborhoods.

It's one of the best events of the year for bringing people together from all over our city and this year was no different with a great, diverse crowd of several hundred.

Our newly elected Democratic mayor, John Cranley, kicked off the event by thanking us and giving a short speech.

Mayor Cranley announced that his focus for the next 4 years was going to be basic services and police. His message was pretty clear: city priorities are safety and basic services [Lon14].

His statement didn't strike me as too unusual until later.

Figure 14.1   Invest in Neighborhoods conference, Cincinnati, OH, 2014.

The first session of the day was a community input session on a city initiative called Plan Cincinnati. Plan Cincinnati is an award-winning development plan to revitalize the city developed under the previous administration [Pla14].

The vision for Plan Cincinnati looks like:

- **Compete:** Be the pivotal economic force of the region.

- **Connect:** Bring people and places together.

- **Live:** Strengthen our magnetic city with energized people.

- **Sustain:** Steward resources and ensure long-term viability.

- **Collaborate:** Partner to reach our common goals.

The plan also contains specific steps for achieving these goals grouped by short term, mid-range, and long-range plans. The plan was developed involving every aspect of the community with a wide cross-section of participation from neighborhoods, community groups, businesses, and citizens.

Great, right?

I thought so too until the coordinator from Plan Cincinnati announced that our job was to prioritize due to limited budget.

Then it started to hit me.

The mayor had already determined his objectives. We weren't here to talk about how to make this plan work and what it would take. Before the session even began, we were told by our new mayor (elected with strong support from the local Chamber of Commerce) that his focus was police and basic services.

Reading between the lines, city money would be going to police and basic services and there would be a small amount of money left over for everything else. We, the people of the city, were there to fight over this amount (or to use the corporate buzzword, "prioritize").

So what did we do? We prioritized. Not that it's bad to have priorities. The problem is that the real priorities had already been determined outside of the community. The conference seemed more like a dog and pony show with the goal of appeasing the community rather than discussing how to make the plan possible.

Instead of investing in an award-winning plan to bring our city into the 21st century, we ended up fighting over which parts of the total plan were most important. Everyone scrambled after the crumbs of the cookie.

To be fair to our newly elected mayor, some of this was determined at the state level years before when the state cut funding to local governments in order to prioritize income tax, estate tax, and business tax cuts (which primarily benefit the wealthy.

Is it any wonder though that people are frustrated by the Democrat/Republican game?

We have a Republican governor and legislature handing out tax breaks to our wealthiest and a newly elected Democratic mayor willing to manage the cuts with zero push back.

What we have is leadership fighting for the interests of the Chamber of Commerce. What we don't have is leadership fighting for a better future for our city.

Thomas Kuhn, in *The Structure of Scientific Revolutions*, described how characteristics of a scientific paradigm determine both the problems to be solved and the realm of possible solutions [Kuh62].

The IIN conference reminded me of Kuhn's description of science where most scientists focus on the problems of a certain paradigm—Newtonian physics, for example—until a new discovery like relativity changes the paradigm. Instead of looking at the needs of our community, figuring out what would be best, and then figuring out how to make it happen, we focused on an extremely limited range of options given to us.

Corporate special interest groups like the Chamber of Commerce set the agenda and priorities: tax breaks and cheap labor. This then "trickles down" to people who have to decide what gets left out, what gets cut. We are given choices—an extremely limited array of choices—mostly for the appearance of participation.

Worse still, it didn't occur to people that the way the process should work is: 1) figure out how to take our city into the 21st century (the Plan Cincinnati team did a great job), and 2) figure out how to get there.

The prioritization process only seems natural if we accept the framing of government as a business. In this framing, spending by government is viewed as an "expense." Government is a "cost center".

In a democracy frame, however, things look quite different. In a democracy, people (through elected representatives) decide what would be best for the country and simultaneously how to get there. In a democracy, people determine what's best for our country.

It's not until you think about the way our country should work, with government representing people and corporations being chartered for the public good that this reverse process, of corporations existing solely for themselves and deciding how little they want to contribute, appears wrong.

The religion of market fundamentalism has been so successful that we cut our benefits, our pay, our schools, and our communities before the heels of groups like the U.S. (and Ohio) Chamber of Commerce.

We also set aside many of our best solutions because they aren't going to be "realistic" given that the very idea of asking corporations and our wealthiest to contribute their fair share to the community has been taken off the table.

As reported by *The Cincinnati Enquirer*, Mayor John Cranley promised two things to business leaders upon becoming Cincinnati's mayor: access and availability.

Josh Pichler writes [Pic14]:

Now it's clear there's been a reset in relations. Cranley meets and talks regularly with executives, including Tom Williams, president of North American Properties and chair of the Cincinnati Business Committee; Scott Robertson, chairman of RCF Group and chair of the Cincinnati Regional Business Committee; and John Barrett, CEO of Western & Southern Financial Group.

Don't get me wrong. Several of the issues city council and our business community are working on are good issues, such as finding efficiencies with the county on shared services and increasing spending with minority-owned businesses.

However, it's also quite apparent that the main priority of the business community isn't investing in a Cincinnati of the future. It's about maximizing individual profits and paying as little on their end in the form of taxes as possible.

Since 1994, according to David Mann, Cincinnati's former mayor and current Vice Mayor, city services have been cut in half [Man14].

In 2010, the state cut roughly $25 million a year from Cincinnati alone in order to provide tax breaks to corporations and wealthy Ohioans. The cuts mostly benefit the top 4%. Similar cuts were made across Ohio. If you make more than $335,000 a year in Ohio, you receive a $6,000 bonus. Ohio's estate tax was also repealed—it only affected those with estates larger than $338,333 [Aka14b].

If you're in the bottom 96%, you see little benefit as any gains are offset by increases in the sales tax or local property taxes.

The net result as you might expect is that the average person pays the same for less services and the wealthy simply pay less. Wealth frees itself from responsibility.

The new normal in our country is that corporate special interest groups and the wealthy tell us what they're willing to pay, and then we, the citizens, fight over the crumbs.

Isn't this backwards?

In a democracy, shouldn't we, the people, be talking about how to make our country better and then figuring out how to get there? Shouldn't corporations exist for the betterment of our country?

14.2   What unites us

The situation that corporate special interest groups want is people fighting each other. They want us competing over what they decide they want to pay, not talking about what would make our country better and figuring out how to get there. They want us dispersed on many fronts. They want us fighting over issues and policy details.

There are many, many good groups in Cincinnati and Ohio working towards change. Many of them were at the IIN conference.

Add to these the thousands of churches in Ohio: the Baptists, the Catholics, the Protestants, the synagogues, the Mormons, the Lutherans, the Presbyterians, the Church of Christ, the Muslims and the evangelical Christians.

Add to these all of the small businesses and business organizations, the local chambers of commerce, the manufacturing groups, the automotive groups, the unions, the bar associations, the architectural societies, the journalist organizations, the regional development groups, and the minority business organizations.

Add to these the philanthropic organizations like the Moose, the Elk, the Rotary clubs, the Kiwanis, the United Way, the Red Cross, all of the various neighborhood foundations. Add the groups fighting for various disease cures like the American Cancer Society, the Red Cross, the Cystic Fibrosis Foundation, and Prevent Blindness Ohio.

Add the museums, the zoos, the Boys and Girls Clubs, the scouting organizations, the YMCA, and YWCA.

The literacy councils, the Society for the Prevention of Cruelty to Animals, the libraries, the health centers, and the hundreds of arts organizations including theatre groups, orchestras, art galleries, and even puppet troupes.

At first, the list looks a bit daunting (and it's not even scratching the surface). There are a lot of interest groups focused around different issues and causes. It would be very easy to see all of these different groups having different goals and agendas.

What they all seem to share is a common belief in democracy. If they all decided to work together for a common cause like democracy, not only would they find they suddenly had more negotiating leverage but they would also find it much easier to achieve their individual goals.

We would all benefit if we were a more democratic society, if we believed more in equality, if we desired a freedom that was more than consumer choice, if we restored our belief in mutual responsibility and if our economy was working better for more people.

Values create a virtual union. Values are what unite us.

I talk about democracy and our virtual union because there is a different system being proposed. This system is the market as a form of government. Competition in this system isn't competition to build a better country for the people who live in the United States. It's competition among people for *lower wages* and *less benefits*.

The vision of America that the Chamber of Commerce has is an America where people fight and compete with each other every day in order to make a few very wealthy people wealthier.

This is why we need to resurrect these common beliefs that sometimes seem like faded distant memories. They are our sense of common cause and common purpose.

Abraham Lincoln closed the Gettysburg Address by saying:

> It is rather for us to be here dedicated to the great task remaining before us—that from these honored dead we take increased devotion to that cause for which they gave the last full measure of devotion—that we here highly resolve that these dead shall not have died in vain—that this nation, under God, shall have a new birth of freedom—and that government of the people, by the people, for the people, shall not perish from the earth.
> — Abraham Lincoln, 1863. [Lin63]

Belief in these simple, common values supports all of the great work that all of these individual groups do on a day-to-day basis (on often extremely limited budgets, I might add).

What unites us are our values.

A different version of America is being proposed where people are supposed to compete against each other for ever smaller amounts in a never-ending race to the bottom.

We can acquiesce and fight along these false divides or we can remember the principles on which our country was founded. We can remember what makes us a union.

I've heard the same frustration Lessig talks about but I also hear again and again, what can I do? What can I really do?

I believe the answer is both easy and difficult. It's easy because none of the steps are particularly difficult. It's difficult because a great deal of money is being spent to encourage what Lessig calls the politics of resignation—making participation in a democracy culturally unacceptable (You're socialist! You're against free markets! You're against all that is holy and good! You're evil! Markets will take care of everything.).

The flip side of this coin is reactionary. The flip side consists primarily of disputing the proposed Ayn Randian vision of America without offering a better vision. This looks like data. Or deconstruction. Or endless irony.

Power should be challenged. If we do nothing but challenge, however, a vacuum of vision exists that is currently being filled by the beliefs of corporate special interest groups like the U.S. Chamber of Commerce.

The good news is that a better vision exists. We just often forget about it in our haste to talk about policies or the cause we support, or we take this vision for granted thinking everyone already shares our beliefs. In fact, it's really more about resurrecting a vision rather than creating anything new.

This vision is of democracy. This vision is of a freedom that goes beyond consumer choice. This vision is of a people who care about each other as well as themselves. This vision is equality and an economy that works for the benefit of everyone, not just a few.

14.3　Key takeaways and actions

In summary, here's fourteen things to remember and take with you:

1. The mind doesn't work like a computer. People make decisions, especially political decisions, based primarily on values and emotion.

2. More often than not, facts are what we use to justify our beliefs.

3. Objections are expressions of emotional need.

4. Our greatest strength is our numbers.

5. Our strategy should reflect our strength.

6. A system for change is more important than any specific change. This means we should be investing as much or more in *how* to make change happen as we do the specific changes we want to happen.

7. Winning someone over is different than winning an argument.

8. If you want to win someone over, you have to like something about that person.

9. Corporate special interest groups are setting the agenda by redefining values. If we want to set the agenda and shift the landscape, we need to focus on teaching values.

10. Politicians react to social change; they don't create it.

11. You likely have more in common with many of the people you're fighting with than you do differences. Direct your anger towards the corporate special interest groups pushing the divide-and-conquer games rather than the people you want to win over.

12. Anyone who is working to shift or accelerate change in the direction of our shared values is an ally. Once I started recognizing my own beliefs and those of others, I found that many people I had thought of as enemies were actually allies or potential allies. Knowing your beliefs will help you break down false divides.

13. In order for democracy (in any form) to happen in our country, we have to first resurrect the value of democracy.

14. If we want to build a big movement, we should pick a big fight (like democracy or freedom or a working economy).

Talk with the people in your group of **51**. What are their values? What do they believe America should look like? Do they believe in democracy? Do they believe in helping others? A working economy?

In the preface, I asked the question: If each of us could pitch in a little bit each day or each week, what would make the biggest difference?

If you do nothing else, remember the "low-hanging fruit":

- Vote

- Convince others of the importance of voting

- Speak about your values

- Focus on people you can win over (ignore the trolls)

- Identify representatives with similar values and vote for those most likely to win

- Share

- Don't take the bait (I know it *feels* good to dress people down with "the truth" but how productive is it?)

- Lift up and encourage

If you want to go further, here's some additional actions:

1. Encourage the groups you are in to support democracy as part of their mission. How could big ideas like democracy and mutual responsibility help your organization? What other groups are fighting for our values? How could your group work with them?

2. Encourage others to play and become more politically active.

3. Get involved with a community, state, or national organization.

4. Encourage your state, local, and national representatives to support democracy and articulate a different and better vision of our country rather than simply fighting at an issue or policy level.

5. Become a party precinct or ward chair. Precinct chairs make decisions about who should run for difference offices given the political landscape in the area.

6. Encourage your group of **51** to teach and tell their stories about shared values.

7. In your personal conversations, remember to start with what you have in common and build a relationship.

8. Tell your story to a larger audience. Write letters to the editor and encourage your local media to print more stories. Talk with the people in your community organizations and groups. Talk with business leaders in the community about the importance of our country and values like mutual responsibility and democracy.

Lawrence Lessig is right that we need a moonshot. His idea is to try to elect candidates from outside the system to make fundamental reform possible. He is raising money to try to accomplish this through a proposed Super PAC to end all Super PACs.

I think its great he's trying something new and different. What do we have to lose?

I think we can do more though.

The way to move the needle in the direction of "we, the people," is to shift the landscape, support the best representatives we have, and work to elect even better representatives to fight for our values.

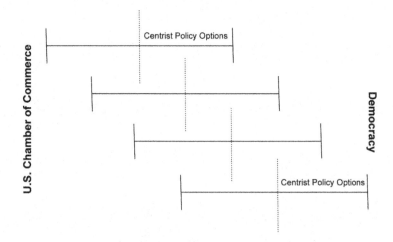

Figure 14.2   Shifting the landscape back towards democracy.

If the landscape shifts, politicians from both parties will follow.

We have a better vision, a vision of a country united for the good of the people. To make this vision reality, we simply need to recognize it, vote it, grow support for it, get our representatives to act on it, and teach it. If enough people fight for this vision, it won't matter what corporate special interest groups want.

All things used to be possible in America. Including the moon.

This is why I completely agree with Lessig that we're not thinking big enough. We're fighting over the crumbs. We're fighting on small tactical issues and policies. We're fighting for bits and pieces here and there.

If we can come together around big ideas like democracy, passing specific policies and legislation will be much easier.

APPENDIX A

REFERENCES AND INDEX

ABOUT THE AUTHOR

I was born and educated in Scotia, New York. During high school, my family moved to Cincinnati, Ohio when General Electric closed part of their operations in Schenectady. As a teenager, I longed to go to Rensselaer Polytechnic Institute, or Cornell, or Clarkson to follow in my father's engineering footsteps.

When I found out-of-state tuition to be too much of a burden, I decided to attend the University of Cincinnati. I completed my undergraduate work in electrical and computer engineering at UC. It was a blessing in disguise.

While attending college, I found myself drawn to the artists, the writers, the economists, the musicians, the physicists, the mathematicians, and the political scientists. I would never have met the same group at an engineering school in New York. I loved the classes about ideas: the math classes, the theory classes, and the liberal arts electives like psychology and sociology. Still, I soldered on towards a Computer Engineering Ph.D.

One summer during graduate school, I found myself with some extra credit hours and enrolled in a couple poetry and fiction classes. This felt like where I belonged. Soon after, I left the Ph.D. program to pursue a degree in English and Comparative Literature. I loved it. Every painful minute of it and it was painful because unlike most of the other graduate students, I had no background in literature. Only a love of reading.

At the time, I wish I would have found more strength from who I was. Instead, I focused on my weaknesses and, after graduating, found myself quite frustrated without a job or clear focus.

I answered a classified ad and took a position as an instructional designer for a company that did technical training. I found I could bridge the gap between sales and engineering because I could speak both languages. This eventually led to a position with one of the largest tech companies in the world. Technical people believe that in order to sell technical products you must understand exactly how a product works. Because of this belief, they often make terrible trainers for the salesforce who just want to know how to sell it.

In the meantime, I wrote. First, for a satirical website called *The Cincinnati Dealer* (a local version of *The Onion*). Then, in 2007, after discovering the work of George Lakoff, I started blogging about politics. Lakoff spoke about a similar problem, talking to people with different beliefs. Blogging introduced me to the netroots community and lead to publication in *The Washington Spectator*, *Daily Kos*, *Alternet*, *Popular Resistance*, and others.

At the same time, my career took off and I found myself designing classes on negotiation, communication, working with difficult people, positioning, presentation, storytelling, and facilitation. I design training for a living and write about politics as a passion.

Employees where I work have access to the best communication and persuasion training in the world. These classes typically cost anywhere from $500 to $2,000 per person for in-person, instructor-led training. Based on my experience, I thought I could design something similar for political conversations in a much more accessible format.

This was the inspiration for *The Little Book of Revolution*, my first book.

Contact

In this book, I've shared what I've learned from my experiences. I view blogging and writing as a conversation. In fact, the best part of blogging is getting to interact with the audience. I find I learn the most from people's comments, suggestions, thoughts, and experiences.

I see this book as the continuation of that conversation.

I'd like to hear your thoughts. If something works for you or you learned something new, please write. If something crashed and burned spectacularly or you have a new perspective, please write.

Through this ongoing dialogue and learning, I hope to find new tales of failure and success.

You can reach me at:

> **E-mail:** akadjian@yahoo.com
> **Twitter:** akadjian
> **Web:** http://www.akadjian.com

I look forward to hearing from you.

-David

REFERENCES

[Aka14a] Akadjian, David. "Why the Pope would be powerful even if he weren't Pope." *Daily Kos.* January 14, 2014. http://www.dailykos.com/story/2014/01/14/1269354/-Why-the-Pope-would-be-powerful-even-if-he-weren-t-Pope

[Aka14b] Akadjian, David. "How Ohio Pulled $4 Billion+ from Communities and Redistributed It Upwards ." *Daily Kos.* Feb. 26, 2014. http://www.dailykos.com/story/2014/02/26/1275645/-How-Ohio-Pulled-4-Billion-from-Communities-and-Redistributed-It-Upwards

[Aka14c] Akadjian, David. "Comcast admits what everyone in a TWC/Comcast market already knows: there is no competition." *Daily Kos.* Apr. 11, 2014. http://www.dailykos.com/story/2014/04/11/1291124/-Comcast-admits-what-everyone-in-a-TWC-Comcast-market-already-knows-there-is-no-competition

[Ale14] "Privatizing Public Education, Higher Ed Policy, and Teachers." *ALEC Exposed.* 2014. http://www.alecexposed.org/wiki/Privatizing_Public_Education,_Higher_Ed_Policy,_and_Teachers

[Ali71] Alinsky, Saul. *Rules for Radicals* New York: Random House, 1971.

[Ana14] Anakai. "Defining 'Freedom' - Who Would YOU Believe?: The Koch Reich or Winston Churchill?" *Daily Kos.* April 21, 2014. http://www.dailykos. com/story/2014/04/21/1293637/-Defining-Freedom-Who-Would-YOU -Believe-The-Koch-Reich-or-Winston-Churchill

[Arb72] Arbib, Michael A. *The metaphorical brain; an introduction to cybernetics as artificial intelligence and brain theory.* New York: Wiley-Interscience, 1972.

[Arr63] Arrow, Kenneth. "Uncertainty and the Welfare Economics of Medical Care." *The American Economic Review.* 53(5), December, 1963, p. 941-973.

[Atk06] Atkins, David. "Why the Right-Wing Gets It—and Why Dems Don't." *Daily Kos.* May 9, 2006. http://www.dailykos.com/story/2006/05/09/ 208784/-Why-the-Right-Wing-Gets-It-and-Why-Dems-Don-t-UPDATED.

[Bac13] Bacon, David. "Chicago Mayor Rahm Emanuel's War on Teachers and Children." *Truthout.* June 20, 2013. http://truth-out.org/news/item/ 17091-chicago-mayor-rahm-emanuels-war-on-teachers-and-children

[Ben12] Bendib, Khalil. "Privatizing Public Schools." *Other Words.* Aug. 6, 2012. http://otherwords.org/privatizing-public-schools-charters-cartoon/

[Ber11] Berg, Andrew G. and Ostry, Jonathan D. "Inequality and Unsustainable Growth: Two Sides of the Same Coin?" *International Monetary Fund.* April 8, 2011. http://www.imf.org/external/pubs/ft/sdn/2011/sdn1108.pdf

[Bla14] Blausen, Bruce. "The Limbic System." Feb. 11, 2014. http://commons. wikimedia.org/wiki/File:Blausen_0614_LimbicSystem.png

[Bib78] *Holy Bible.* New International Version. Grand Rapids, MI: International Bible Society, 1978.

[Bos03] Bosworth, Michael T. and Holland, John R. *Customer Centric Selling.* New York: McGraw-Hill, 2003.

[Bot12] de Botton, Alain. *Religion for Atheists: A Non-Believer's Guide to the Uses of Religion.* New York: Vintage Books, 2012.

[Bre12] Brewer, Joe. "The REAL Reason Conservatives Always Win." *Cognitive Policy Works.* June 22, 2012. http://www.cognitivepolicyworks.com/ blog/2012/06/22/the-real-reason-conservatives-always-win/

[Bud14] Budget of the United States Government Fiscal Year 2014. "Historical Tables: Table 2.1—Receipts by Source: 1934-2019" 2014. http://www.whitehouse.gov/omb/budget/Historicals

[Can14] "How the Working Families Party is Already Changing Electoral Politics." *The Nation.* July 7, 2014. http://www.thenation.com/article/180314/ how-working-families-party-already-changing-electoral-politics

[CDC63] "Child with Measles." *Center for Disease Control.* 1963. http://phil. cdc.gov/phil/quicksearch.asp Image: 1152

[Cen14] "United States Census Bureau USA QuickFacts." United States Census Bureau, 2014. http://quickfacts.census.gov/qfd/states/00000.html

[CoC14] "Economic and Tax Policy Division." *U.S. Chamber of Commerce.* 2014. https://www.uschamber.com/economic-policy

[Cha10] Chang, Ha-Joon. *23 Things They Don't Tell You About Capitalism.* New York: Bloomsbury Press, 2010.

[Che12] Chen, Adrian. "The awful cover letter all of Wall Street is laughing about." *Gawker.* Feb. 9, 2012. http://gawker.com/5883684/the-awful-cover-letter-all-of-wall-street-is-laughing-about

[Coh90] Cohen, Allan R. and Bradford, David L. *Influence Without Authority* New York: John Wiley & Sons, 1990.

[Col09] Collins, Loren. "The Truth About Tytler." *LorenCollins.net.* Jan. 25, 2009. http://www.lorencollins.net/tytler.html

[Cos06] Costandi, Mo. Exorcising Animal Spirits: "The Discovery of the Nerve Function." *Neurophilosophy.* November 11, 2006. http://neurophilosophy. wordpress.com/2006/11/16/exorcising-animal-spirits-the-discovery -of-nerve-function/

[Cou04] Coulter, Ann. *How to Talk to a Liberal (If You Must).* New York: Random House, 2004.

[Cre14] Cressman, Derek. *Money in Politics: Candidate Forum.* Moderated by Marge Baker. Netroots Nation, 2014.

[Dal12] Dal Vera, Rocco et al. facilitators. *Influencing Without Authority* Xavier Leadership Center Training, 2012.

[Dau01] Daugman, John. "Brain metaphor and brain theory." *Philosophy and the Neurosciences,* Chapter 2, Ed. by W. Bechtel et al., Oxford: Blackwell Publishers, 2001.

[Des72] Descartes, René. *Treatise on Man.* Trans. by T. Hall. Cambridge, MA: Harvard University Press, 1972.

[Dil41] Dillard, Irving. *Mr. Justice Brandeis, Great American.* Saint Louis: The Modern View Press, 1941.

[Dou11] Doughery, Kevin D. et al. *The Values and Beliefs of the American Public.* Baylor University, September, 2011. http://www.baylor.edu/content/ services/document.php/153501.pdf

[Dyl67] Dylan, Bob. "All Along the Watchtower." *John Wesley Harding.* Columbia Records, 1967.

[Ein49] Einstein, Albert. "Why Socialism?" *Monthly Review.* May 1949. http://monthlyreview.org/2009/05/01/why-socialism/

[Eng60] Engel, Carl. "Jacquard Loom." Deutsches Museum - Textiltechnik. Nordlingen, 1860. http://en.wikipedia.org/wiki/History_of_ silk#mediaviewer/File:DMM_29263ab_Jacquardwebstuhl.jpg

[Ess10] Esseltine, Charles & Adrienne. "Bricks of Character." Apr. 10, 2010. https://www.flickr.com/photos/94246383@N00/4523048070/

[Fis13] Fischer, Will and Huang, Chye-Ching. "Mortgage Interest Deduction is Ripe for Reform." Center on Budget and Policy Priorities. June, 25, 2013. http://www.cbpp.org/cms/?fa=view&id=3948

[Fit09] Fitzpatrick, Erik. "Ayn Rand Institute." Oct. 4, 2009. https://www.flickr.com/photos/22244945@N00/3983330014/

[Fra04] Frank, Thomas. "What's the Matter with Kansas?" New York: Henry Holt and Company, LLC, 2004.

[Fra10] Franzen, Jonathan. *Freedom*. New York: Farrar, Straus and Giroux, 2010.

[Fre14] "Animal icons." *Freepik.com*. 2014. http://www.freepik.com

[Fri02] Friedman, Milton. *Capitalism and Freedom: Fortieth Anniversary Edition*. Chicago: The University of Chicago Press, 2002.

[Fri04] Friedman, Joel and Shapiro, Isaac. "Tax Returns: A Comprehensive Assessment of the Bush Administration's Record on Cutting Taxes." Center on Budget and Policy Priorities. April 24, 2004. http://www.cbpp.org/files/4-23-04tax.pdf

[Fre89] Freud, Sigmund. "The Neuroses of Defense." *The Freud Reader*. Ed. Gay, Peter. New York: Norton, 1989.

[Gal13] Galazzo. "Backpropagation Network." Aug. 2, 2013. http://developer.nokia.com/community/wiki/File:NeuralNetwork.png

[Gal93] Gallant, Stephen I. *Neural Network Learning and Expert Systems* Cambridge: MIT Press, 1994.

[Gat13] Gates, Gary J. and Newport, Frank. "Gallup Special Report: New Estimates of the LGBT Population in the United States." The Williams Institute, February 2013. http://williamsinstitute.law.ucla.edu/research/census-lgbt-demographics-studies/gallup-lgbt-pop-feb-2013/

[Gil14] Gilens, Martin and Page, Benjamin I., "Testing Theories of American Politics: Elites, Interest Groups, and Average Citizens." *Perspectives in Politics*, Fall 2014.

[Gly10] Glynn, Ian. *Elegance in Science*. Oxford: Oxford University Press, 2010.

[Gold04] Goldstein, Patrick. "The Big Picture: Political insider's new script." *Los Angeles Times*. August 24, 2004. http://articles.latimes.com/2004/aug/24/entertainment/et-goldstein24.

[Gra13] Graeber, David. *The Democracy Project*. New York: Spiegal & Grau, 2013.

[Gre07] Greenwald, Glenn. "Bad Stenographers." *Salon*. November 28, 2007. http://www.salon.com/2007/11/28/stenography/.

[Gri65] *Griswold v. Connecticut*. 381 U.S. 479. June 7, 1965. http://www.law.cornell.edu/supremecourt/text/381/479

[Har68] Hardin, Garrett. "The Tragedy of the Commons." *Science* 162 (3859), 1968, p. 1243-1248. http://www.sciencemag.org/content/162/3859/1243.full.pdf

[Har01] Harnden, Toby. "Uncle wrestles shark to save boy's severed arm." *The Telegraph.* Jul. 9, 2001. http://www.telegraph.co.uk/news/worldnews/northamerica/usa/1333379/Uncle-wrestles-shark-to-save-boys-severed-arm.html

[Har10] Hartman, Thom. *Unequal Protection.* San Francisco: Berrett-Koehler, 2010.

[Har38] Harris & Ewing. Washington Votes. Library of Congress Prints and Photographs Division. 1938. http://www.loc.gov/pictures/item/hec2009011227/

[Hay12] Hayes, Christopher. *The Twilight of the Elites* New York: Random House, 2012.

[Hay13] Hayes, Christopher. "All in with Chris Hayes." *NBC News* November 1, 2013. http://www.nbcnews.com/id/53457710/ns/msnbc-all-in-with-chris_hayes/

[Hea10] Heath, Joseph. *Economics Without Illusions: Debunking the Myths of Modern Capitalism.* New York: Random House, 2010.

[Her09] Hertzberg, Hendrik. *One Million.* New York: Harry N. Abrams, 2009.

[Hil00] Hillel the Elder. *Ethics of our Fathers.* 1:14. http://www.chabad.org/library/article_cdo/aid/680274/jewish/Ethics-of-the-Fathers-Pirkei-Avot.html

[Hod52] Hodgkin, A.L. and Huxley, A.F. "A quantitative description of membrane current and its application to conduction and excitation in nerve." *The Journal of Physiology*, 117 (1952), p. 500-544.

[HUD13] Department of Housing and Urban Development. "FY 2013 Budget: Housing and Communities Built to Last." http://portal.hud.gov/hudportal/documents/huddoc?id=CombBudget2013.pdf

[IDS09] IDS Photos. "Time to score, collecting arrows and scoring at Dunster Archery competition, Somerset, 2009." June 14, 2009.

[Jam90] James, William. "Psychology (Briefer Course): Association" *Neurocomputing: Foundations of Research.* Anderson, James A. and Rosenfeld, Edward Eds. Cambridge: MIT Press, 1988.

[Jef98] Jefferson, Thomas. "Letter to the Danbury Baptists." *Library of Congress Information Bulletin.* Vol. 57, No. 6. June, 1998. http://www.loc.gov/loc/lcib/9806/danpre.html

[Jim13] Jimenez, Edgar. "Pope Francis among the people at St. Peter's Square." May 12, 2013. http://en.wikipedia.org/wiki/File:Pope_Francis_among_the_people_at_St._Peter%27s_Square_-_12_May_2013.jpg

[Kir89] Kirk, Marshall and Madsen, Hunter. *After the Ball: How America Will Conquer Its Fear & Hatred of Gays in the 90s.* New York: Doubleday, 1989.

[Kos09] Kosmin, Barry A. and Keysar, Ariela. "American Religious Identification Survey (ARIS 2008) Summary Report." Trinity College, 2008.

http://www.scribd.com/doc/17136871/American-Religious-Identification-Survey-ARIS-2008-Summary-Report

[Kuh62]   Kuhn, Thomas. *The Structure of Scientific Revolutions.* Chicago: University Press, 1962.

[Kru94]   Krugman, Paul. *Peddling Prosperity: Economic Sense and Nonsense in the Age of Diminished Expectations.* New York: Norton, 1994.

[Lak04]   Lakoff, George. *Don't Think of an Elephant: Know Your Values and Frame the Debate.* New York: Chelsea Green, 2004.

[Lak06]   Lakoff, George. *Whose Freedom? The Battle over America's Most Important Idea.* New York: Farrar, Strauss, and Giroux, 2006.

[Lak08]   Lakoff, George. *The Political Mind: Why You Can't Understand 21st Century Politics with an 18th Century Brain.* New York: Penguin, 2008.

[Lav83]   Lavater, Johann Kaspar. "Four humours - image of woodcut." *Physiognomische Fragmente zur Beförderung von Menschenkenntniss und Menschenliebe.* 1783.

[Law04]   Lawless, Andrew "Status Anxiety - An Interview with Alain de Botton." Three Monkey's Online (TMO) Magazine. August 1, 2004. http://www.threemonkeysonline.com/status-anxiety-an-interview-with-alain-de-botton/

[Len94]   Lenoir, Timothy. "Helmholtz and the Materialities of Communication." *Program in History and Philosophy of Science.* Stanford University, 1994.

[Les11]   Lessig, Lawrence. *Republic, Lost: How Money Corrupts Congress—and a Plan to Stop It.* New York: Twelve, 2011.

[Les14]   Lessig, Lawrence. "Campaign Finance and the Nihilist Politics of Resignation." *The Atlantic.* Apr. 10, 2014. http://www.theatlantic.com/politics/archive/2014/04/campaign-finance-and-the-nihilist-politics-of-resignation/360437/

[Lev11]   Levine, Bruce. *Get Up, Stand Up: Uniting Populists, Energizing the Defeated, and Battling the Corporate Elite.* Vermont: Chelsea Green, 2011.

[Lev11]   Levine, Bruce. "How Ayn Rand Seduced Generations of Young Men and Helped Make the U.S. Into a Selfish, Greedy Nation." *Alternet.* December 15, 2011. http://www.alternet.org/story/153454/how_ayn_rand_seduced_generations_of_young_men_and_helped_make_the_u.s._into_a_selfish,_greedy_nation

[Lin63]   Lincoln, Abraham. *The Gettysburg Address.* Abraham Lincoln Online. Gettysburg, PA. Nov. 19, 1863. http://www.abrahamlincolnonline.org/lincoln/speeches/gettysburg.htm

[Lip56]   Lipsey, R.G. and Lancaster, Kelvin. "The General Theory of Second Best." *The Review of Economic Studies.* 24(1), 1956-57. p. 11-32.

[Llo11]   Lloyd, John. "Seen on the street in Chelan, Washington." Jun. 17, 2011. https://www.flickr.com/photos/32109282@N00/5980815126/

[Loc97] Locke, John ed. Woolhouse, Roger. *An Essay Concerning Human Understanding*. New York: Penguin Books, 1997.

[Lon14] London, John. "Mayor John Cranley unveils Cincinnati's budget plan." *WLWT Channel 5*. May 14, 2014. http://www.wlwt.com/news/Mayor-John-Cranley-unveils-Cincinnati-s-budget-plan/25984252

[Luc13] Luckhardt, Fritz. "Woman kissing her reflection in the looking glass." Boston Public Library. Sept. 25, 2013. https://www.flickr.com/photos/boston_public_library/11968910755/

[Lur13] Lurie, Stephen. "Why Doesn't the Constitution Guarantee the Right to Education?" *The Atlantic*. Oct. 16, 2013. http://www.theatlantic.com/education/archive/2013/10/why-doesnt-the-constitution-guarantee-the-right-to-education/280583/

[MA14] "Constitution of the Commonwealth of Massachusetts." *Commonwealth of Massachusetts*. 2014. https://malegislature.gov/Laws/Constitution

[Mac14] "The Overton Window." Mackinac Center for Public Policy, 2014. http://www.mackinac.org/OvertonWindow

[Mad00] Madison, James. *The Writings of James Madison*. Ed. Gaillard Hunt. New York: G.P. Putnams Sons, 1900. http://oll.libertyfund.org/titles/1933

[Mag04] Magie, L.J. "Game Board." *United States Patent and Trademark Office*. PN#748626. Jan. 5, 1904. http://patft.uspto.gov/netahtml/PTO/index.html

[Mah14] Maher, Bill. "New Rules: Dead Man's Party (The Power of Language)." Real Time with Bill Maher. March 21, 2014. https://www.youtube.com/watch?v=9rRLoTbKDa0

[Man14] Mann, David. "Cincinnati City Government—Past, Present, and Future: Vice Mayor David Mann Reflects on City Hall Then and Now." *AIR Inc*. January 16, 2014. http://www.airinc.org/communityforum.html

[Mcc14] McConnell, Mitch. "EPA's new plan to target greenhouse gases will kill jobs, devastate middle class." *Fox News*. June 2, 2014. http://www.foxnews.com/opinion/2014/06/02/epa-new-plan-to-target-greenhouse-gases-will-kill-jobs-devastate-middle-class/

[Mci96] McIntyre, Robert S. "Tax Expenditures—The Hidden Entitlements." *Citizens for Tax Justice*. May, 1996. http://www.ctj.org/pdf/hident.pdf

[Mck11] McKibben, Bill. "The Gang That Couldn't Lobby Straight." *Huffington Post*. March 22, 2011. http://www.huffingtonpost.com/bill-mckibben/the-gang-that-couldnt-lob_b_839047.html

[Meh71] Mehrabian, Albert. *Silent Messages: Implicit Communication of Emotions and Attitudes* Belmont, CA: Wadsworth Publishing, 1971.

[Moon12] Mooney, Chris. *The Republican Brain: The Science of Why They Deny Science—and Reality* Hoboken, New Jersey: Wiley, 2012.

[Moon14] Mooney, Chris. "Study: You Can't Change an Anti-Vaxxer's Mind," *Mother Jones*. March 3, 2014. http://www.motherjones.com/ environment/2014/02/vaccine-denial-psychology-backfire-effect

[Moy01] Moyer, Bill et. al. *Doing Democracy: The MAP Model for Organizing Social Movements* British Columbia: New Society Publishers, 2001.

[Mye04] Myers, D.G. "Theories of Emotion." *Psychology: Seventh Edition*. New York: Worth Publishers, 2004.

[Nag13] Nagourney, Adam. "A defiant rancher savors the audience that rallied to his side." NY Times. April 23, 2014. http://www.nytimes.com/2014/04/24/ us/politics/rancher-proudly-breaks-the-law-becoming-a-hero-in- the-west.html

[Nad13] Nader, Ralph. "10 Books to Provoke Conversation in the New Year." Huffington Post. December 31, 2013. http://www.huffingtonpost.com/ ralph-nader-2014-book-recommendations_b_4524616.html

[Nyh10] Nyhan, Brendan and Reifler, Jason. "When Corrections Fail: The Persistence of Political Misperceptions." *Political Behavior* 32(2) p. 303-330.

[Oba13] Obama, Barack. "Remarks by the President on Economic Mobility." *White House*. December 4, 2013. http://www.whitehouse.gov/the-press-office/ 2013/12/04/remarks-president-economic-mobility

[Pic14] Pichler, Josh. "Cranley teams up with CEOs, outlines priorities." *Cincinnati Enquirer*. Mar. 5, 2014. http://www.cincinnati.com/story/money/ josh-pichler/2014/02/15/cranley-teams-up-with-ceos-outlines- priorities/5524235/

[Pik14] Piketty, Thomas. *Capital in the Twenty-First Century*. Cambridge: The Belknap Press, 2014.

[Pla14] *Plan Cincinnati*. City of Cincinnati. http://www.plancincinnati.org/

[Pol45] Pólya, George. *How to Solve It: A New Aspect of Mathematical Method*. Princeton, NJ: Princeton University Press, 1945.

[Pop13] Pope Francis. *Evangelii Gaudium (or Apostolic Exhortation)*. Nov. 24, 2013. http://apps.washingtonpost.com/g/page/politics/pope-francis- denounces-economic-inequality-consumerism/619/

[Pou92] Poundstone, William *Prisoner's Dilemma: John von Neumann, Game Theory and the Puzzle of the Bomb*. New York: Doubleday, 1992.

[Pow71] Powell, Lewis. "Confidential Memorandum: Attack of American Free Enterprise System." *The Powell Memo* (also known as *The Powell Manifesto*) August 23, 1971. http://reclaimdemocracy.org/powell_memo_lewis/

[Pug77] Pugh, George Edgin. *The Biological Origin of Human Values*. New York: Routledge & Kegan Paul, 1977.

[Ran66] Rand, Ayn et al. *Capitalism: the Unknown Ideal*. New York: Signet, 1966.

[Ran60] Rand, Ayn. "Faith and Force: The Destroyers of the Modern World." *Philosophy: Who Needs It (The Ayn Rand Library Vol. 1)*. New York: Signet Books, 1984.

[Rea81] Reagan, Ronald. "Address To The Nation On The Program For Economic Recovery." *Social Security Administration – Presidential Statements*. Sept. 24, 1981. http://www.socialsecurity.gov/history/reaganstmts.html

[Rec14] "Our Hidden History of Corporations in the United States." *Reclaiming Democracy*. 2014. http://reclaimdemocracy.org/corporate-accountability-history-corporations-us/

[Rei05] Reitman, Jason, director. *Thank You for Smoking*. Room9 Entertainment et al., 2005.

[Roc43] "Freedom from Want." *Saturday Evening Post*. Mar. 6, 1943.

[Roo41] Roosevelt, Franklin D. "Four freedoms speech." Annual Message to Congress on State of the Union. FDR library. January 6, 1941. http://www.fdrlibrary.marist.edu/pdfs/fftext.pdf

[Rou02] Rousseau, Jeans-Jacques. *The Social Contract* and *The First and Second Discourses*. Ed. Susan Dunn. New Haven: Yale University Press, 2002.

[Row13] "20 Quotes on Writing by J.K. Rowling." *Azvedos Reviews*. June 23, 2013. http://www.azevedosreviews.com/2013/06/23/jk-rowlings-20-quotes-on-writing/

[Roy13] Roy, Ananya. "Who is Dependent on Welfare." *The #GlobalPOV Project*. Dec. 3, 2013. https://www.youtube.com/watch?v=-rtySUhuokM

[Sea34] Seattle Municipal Archives. "Broadway looking north from Thomas." Item No. 8760. Mar. 23, 1934. https://www.flickr.com/photos/seattlemunicipalarchives/4017399792/

[Sher42] Sherrington, C.S. *Man on his nature*. Cambridge: Cambridge University Press, 1942.

[Sur05] Surowiecki, James. *The Wisdom of Crowds*. New York: Doubleday, 2004.

[Tan07] Tang, Huajin, Tan, Kay Chen and Yi, Zhang. *Neural Networks: Computational Models and Applications*. New York: Springer-Verlag, 2007.

[UN14] "The Universal Declaration of Human Rights." *United Nations*. Dec. 10, 1948. http://www.un.org/en/documents/udhr/

[Ung75] Unger, Roberto Mangabeira. *Knowledge and Politics*, New York: Free Press, 1975.

[Viz11] Vizu, Victor. "Crossroad in winter." Jan. 14, 2011. http://commons.wikimedia.org/wiki/File:Crossroad_in_winter_2.jpg

[Wal93] Wallace, David Foster. "E Unibus Pluram: Television and U.S. Fiction." *Review of Contemporary Fiction*. 13:2 Summer, 1993.

[Wat95] "Watt's Steam Engine." *Meyers Großes Konversations-Lexikon*. 1885-90. http://commons.wikimedia.org/wiki/File:Dampfma_gr.jpg

[Wes06] Westen, Drew et. al. "Neural Bases of Motivated Reasoning: An fMRI Study of Emotional Constraints on Partisan Political Judgment in the 2004 U.S. Presidential Election." *Journal of Cognitive Neuroscience*, 18:11 (2006), p. 1947-1958.

[Wes07] Westen, Drew. *The Political Brain: The Role of Emotion in Deciding the Fate of the Nation*, New York: Perseus, 2007.

[Wil13] Willis, Oliver. "Pope Francis Rebukes 'Marxist' Attack from Rush Limbaugh & Conservative Media." *Media Matters*. Dec. 15, 2013. http://mediamatters.org/blog/2013/12/15/pope-francis-rebukes-marxist-attack-from-rush-1/197273

[Win08] Winfrey, Oprah. "Stanford University 2008 Commencement Speech." Stanford News. June 15, 2008. Transcript: http://news.stanford.edu/news/2008/june18/como-061808.html. Video: http://www.youtube.com/watch?v=Bpd3raj8xww&feature=kp.

[Win13] Winship, Michael. "Campaign Cash Rules Drown in the Bathtub." *Moyers & Company*. Dec. 23, 2013. http://billmoyers.com/2013/12/23/campaign-cash-rules-drown-in-the-bathtub/

[Wol12] Wolf, Naomi. "The NDAA: a clear and present danger to American liberty." *The Guardian*. Feb. 29, 2012. http://www.theguardian.com/commentisfree/cifamerica/2012/feb/29/ndaa-danger-american-liberty

[Wol12] Wolff, E. N. *The Asset Price Meltdown and the Wealth of the Middle Class*. New York: New York University, 2012.

[Wri02] Wright, Keith. "President George W. Bush waves from Air Force One." *DefenseImagery.mil* 020429-F-MJ378-015. Apr. 29, 2002.

[Ygl14] Yglesias, Matthew. "The short guide to Capital in the 21st Century." *Vox*. June 3, 2014. http://www.vox.com/2014/4/8/5592198/the-short-guide-to-capital-in-the-21st-century

Index

CPSIA information can be obtained
at www.ICGtesting.com
Printed in the USA
BVOW03s2011251116

468707BV00008B/42/P